RYAN GEORGE

SCARED TO LIFE

TALES OF A GOOD GOD WHO REVEALS
HIS HEART WHEN OURS IS RACING

ISBN Paperback: 978-1-955051-07-1

ISBN eBook: 978-1-955051-08-8

Design by Vanessa Mendozzi

CONTENTS

ACKNOWLEDGMENTS

To Woody Torrence.
Thanks for setting the pace, the direction, and the example.

SOVEREIGN FACTORY SETTINGS

Redemption isn't always necessary.

I wrote this book for the wrong reason.

I used to think I had to redeem my adventures, especially my adrenaline rushes. I felt ashamed to go bungee jumping in South Africa while my friends spent their vacation days on dusty streets, working with rescued victims of human trafficking. I felt embarrassed that I went to Nepal—not to mentor students my church supported but to play in the skies above the Himalayan Mountains. I wrestled with whether or not the spiritual moments I had experienced in the Arctic Circle or on helicopter expeditions or during aerobatic flights were worth what I had spent to enjoy them.

While Jesus walked on water during a storm, his biographers didn't mention whether or not he liked to surf. There's no account of Jesus kayaking the Jordan River after a good rain or jumping off a mountain under a nylon wing. A whisper in me said he wouldn't have spent his evenings in an ultralight, his Saturdays in a race car, or his sabbaticals on Canadian glacier treks.

I know where that line of thinking started in me.

As a high school student, I wanted to work in automotive design, marketing, or journalism. I lived on a beach highway where 250,000 cars passed my house on summer weekends, and I studied the vehicles that passed our front yard. I read and re-read my grandpa's hand-me-down *Popular Mechanics*. I went to the library to devour *Car & Driver*, *Motor Trend*, and *Road & Track*. I designed scores of vehicle concepts, one of which became standard issue on Ford F-150 pickups while I was in college.

My pastor during those years told me that my passion was materialistic—specifically, that there would be no cars in heaven. His exact words are probably true. I mean, those gold streets deserve better than tire marks. But his sentiment left its mark on my soul. What I heard was, "Ryan, what interests you doesn't interest God."

Fast forward about a decade through four out-of-state moves to 2006. I joined the parking lot greeter team at my new church, where I quickly memorized the names, stories, and parking preferences of the folks that went with specific vehicles. I was part of a team that made our megachurch seem smaller and more intimate—at least more personable. I could help drivers feel seen when I asked them about their cars, their license plates, or their window stickers. Within a few years, I led one of the parking lot teams. That allowed me to tend a spiritual incubator, where almost-believers and new followers of Christ fell in love with Jesus.

Fast forward again—this time to 2014. I got to represent MINI's marketing team—first in developing the concept for a TV commercial and then on media day at the New York International Auto Show, where they introduced it. After spending two weekends with automotive advertisers and journalists, pushing a car to its limits and seeing covers pulled off brand new models in front of the press, I recognized what Jesus had done. He had given me a taste of my teenage dreams—enough to know he'd given me a better life than I had imagined but also let me revel in living out those original dreams for a few days. I realized that Jesus had fulfilled my high school aspirations in my church's parking lots—far from Detroit or New York or Los Angeles—in the Blue Ridge Mountains I love so much.

Shortly after the tragedy of George Floyd's murder in 2020, two of my pastors interviewed one of the Black senior saints in our church on stage and let him ask them hard questions in return. At one point in the public conversation, Woody asked Melvin what had helped him and his wife feel welcomed and comfortable in our predominantly white church. Dr. Pride referenced an early encounter with Woody's mom and then added, "The parking team here." I was sitting on the front row, and Woody looked at me like no pastor ever has. I can't recall if I got a lump in my throat and moist eyes at that moment—or just right now while remembering it.

What I did know after that moment was that what interested me also interested God.

See, my passion for everything about cars wasn't redeemed. It didn't have to be. It was hard-wired into a skinny kid who lived on the southern side of an eastbound highway. Jesus wanted me to hang out with people around cars—ministering to them directly or preparing their hearts for a holy encounter inside the church building. And so,

almost every Sunday morning of my 30s and 40s has been spent in
parking lots. I'm still as enamored as ever by the lines and designs of
cars and trucks and SUVs. But now I know they weren't meant to be
my profession—just the accoutrement of my calling.

Those fifteen seconds, as I sat with legs crossed on the floor below
Melvin and my pastors on stage, held the first of two indelible moments
that assured me this book could be more than an insecure highlight
reel. The other one happened after I had written all of the chapters of
this manuscript and had scrapped the original introduction.

See, while writing this book, I read this book. In addition to reliving
these fantastic moments and realizations, these chapters reminded me
of what's not in here:

- hearts downloading to each other after the euphoria wore off
- cards and text messages from dudes after we got back to our
  respective homes
- requests from friends to take their husbands on the next adventure
- breakfast table discussions where tales were told and retold
- smaller explorations big enough only for my journal

Oh, and one particular moment that needed to be added—the second
of those two glimpses into the heart behind this book.

I had just gone through a season where I had learned (the hard
way) about the prudence of asking Jesus for his permission instead
of his blessing. As I wrestled with the dream of going to Antarctica,
I went for a prayer walk in our subdivision. "God, I want to go, but I
don't want to spend this money if you don't want me to." I told Jesus
that I looked forward to finding him in Antarctica, to seeing his glory
there—but only if he *wanted* me to go. I vividly remember what the

sky looked like as I looked up into it and told Jesus about my dream. I chuckle now because he knew that dream better than I did or ever will.

I had stopped walking and was standing at a bend in a road named Crystal Lane when the answer came back crystal-clear. This sounds weird, but I didn't just sense "yes" or "go." I heard it in the way a grandfather smiles, almost laughing, when he says you can drive his boat, his truck, or his tractor. As I sped down the hill to our house to book the tickets, it was as if he called from where I'd been standing, "I'll see you there!"

And he did. Some of the conversations on that Antarctica trip left a cumulative mark on my soul.

What I've come to realize about physical adventures and even adrenaline rushes is that I don't have to bring Jesus into any of them. He's already there. He has probably been waiting for me at each one. I picture him patting his knees and standing when I arrive. "Oh, good! You made it. Let's get going."

Jesus designed my adrenal system. He scheduled my birth for when bungee jumping and paragliding would be commercial ventures and when I could use Google to find vendors to do them. The Holy Spirit knew the men who would enter my life and what a shared adventure would do for our hearts, our relationships, and our respective ministries. The Father knew the prayers I'd offer beforehand and the worship I'd exclaim afterward. He knew I would see him, recognize his movement, and want to share what I saw.

God has shown me that the greatest adventures start with Advent—his arrival, his participation, and his infusions. Jesus, for sure, redeems many things: pain and trauma, loss and even poor choices. He doesn't waste a teachable moment, a horrible tragedy, or an unfinished story. He flexes his sovereignty and flashes his compassion in those redemptive narratives. But what I've found—and what you're about to read in the following pages—is that he can leverage our passions too. He can align circumstances to how he programmed us at the factory. He can reveal himself at any time, in any place, to anyone.

And I hope in the paragraphs of this book, he likewise reveals his heart and his character to you.

SCARED TO LIFE

Peace might look different than you think.

I am embarrassingly skilled at moving individual and group conversations to stories of my adventures. I work to redeem that tendency by (1) making those tales entertaining and (2) explaining interesting aspects that spectators might not know. And I try to inspire my conversation partners in those discussions to lean into their fears.

One of the interjections I hear back in those conversations is, "Not me. I'd be scared to death."

I can relate to that rebuttal. Death scares me, especially by the pain that typically accompanies it. My hands sweat profusely when my Airbus, Boeing, or Embraer shakes with turbulence. One of the reasons I've not been able to chase bigger whitewater dreams is that

I freak the heck out when I'm upside down in my kayak—even in calm sections of the rivers I frequent. Since an incident in college, when I and the driver both woke up while her car was doing highway speeds down the median, I haven't been able to sleep in a car while someone else is driving. I remember when the Bolivian equivalent of DEA agents interrogated me in a language that I didn't speak on my first morning ever in South America. One of the agents had both of his hands in ready-to-engage positions on his assault rifle while the other guy in camo studied my passport and my face and then my passport again. I was the only American within probably a half mile; nobody was looking for me or heading my way. I don't remember if what I feared was death, but I definitely feared what might come next.

So, I understand why friends and strangers categorically rule out certain adventures. I have empathy when I reply that embracing my fears scares me too—to life.

Something grows in my heart after my hands stop shaking or sweating. Something explodes within my rib cage after it finishes heaving from anxious breathing. Then come the victory hoots and the hollers of conquest. My insecurities disappear for a while after I get out of an appreciated safety harness. Concerns about my business, my family, and my future temporarily lose their places in the rotation of my thoughts while I'm standing on ground I just landed on. This sounds weird, but I feel Heaven smile on me in those moments. The euphoria that comes with each adrenaline rush feels like a rare and precious gift from a good and generous God. The sky feels bigger. My fears feel like a distant memory.

I feel fully and utterly alive.

The day before I started writing this chapter, I finished an intro- spective retreat in the high desert of Southern California. After some conversations with its host, Bob Goff, I had wrestled with profound questions about my identity, my influence, and my assumptions. This tension was good and productive, but I needed to clear my head for a bit. I craved a system cleanse, especially if it came with an adrenal dump. Thankfully, about thirty miles from Bob's fire pits and rocking chairs, I found a soaring operation that offered aerobatic flights.

Soaring uses fixed-wing gliders that are usually towed up by a powered aircraft to the desired launch elevation. (For us, it was 7,800 feet.) There, the majestic gliders with their long white wings unhook from their tow vehicles and begin their gradual descent back to the runway. Or they detach and drop into a series of rolls and loops, spins and stalls.

The other soaring flights I've enjoyed came by way of soaring clubs whose pilots weren't allowed to take paying passengers upside down. But on this afternoon, I was riding with Garret Willat, a three-time national champion aerobatic pilot. When I walked up to the cockpit, he handed me a parachute. I wasn't expecting that. I definitely hadn't mentally prepared for this possibility.

"Do you know how to use one of these?" he asked.

"I've used one before," I answered.

"Good. It's pretty simple. You pull this tab here to release the canopy. When you're clear of the glider, you pull this ring here to release the chute." He explained that if we did need to eject, it'd probably be while the sailplane was upside down.

"Have you ever needed to use this?" I asked.

"Never," he replied.

You'd think that answer would calm my nerves when we started hitting desert thermals behind an old crop duster. It didn't. For whatever reason, turbulence scares me more than barrel rolls. The fear didn't end there with the thermals, though. At one point in the dash video, you can hear the wind grow silent and a haunting whistle take its place. Hanging upside down in my harness, you can hear me ask, "What's that?"

"It's us. Stopping."

Garret had stalled us upside down.

In all the crazy things I've ever done in the sky, that was a first. It's as surreal as you're probably imagining right now. I don't know if it's fortunate or unfortunate, but that moment lasted maybe two seconds. Immediately after Garret's succinct answer, we fell out of the sky with the nose pointing straight at the desert floor. Garret pulled the maneuver again in a mix of rolls and loops and zero-G parabolas before we got down to 1,500 feet off the hard deck. Under that elevation, he wasn't allowed to perform inversions.

"Do you like drag racing?" Garret asked. I looked over, and we were gliding parallel with a rural highway—maybe thirty feet off the ground, passing a pickup that was hauling through the desert. I pumped my fist. "Yes!" I exclaimed. I shouted and pumped both fists. "WOOOOO!" By my count later from the dash cam footage, we had been upside down a dozen times. I didn't know that as we slid onto the runway and squeaked to a stop, but euphoria jiggled inside my harness. I didn't need a number to tell me what I had just seen and felt and fully known.

Had I been utterly scared? Yes. My hands were sweaty. My armpits too. Some of my buddies laugh because that Facebook video included the first and last times they have ever heard me swear.

But life coursed through my veins. It throbbed in both my literal heart and figurative one. Gratitude swelled in my chest and escaped in large exhales.

After this adrenaline rush, I felt ready to confront the giants with which I had wrestled at The Oaks Center with Bob. I wasn't just scared to life. I was scared into action, into living. Embracing that discomfort didn't just lead to a flood of rewarding body chemicals. Per usual, it opened me to worship and creativity and resolve. Some of my most productive afternoons of blogging and evenings of writing book chapters have come after a morning with an elevated heart rate and internal sirens. I find creative flow after I scare my excuses away, after I shock my inhibitions into retreat. When all of the warning lights on the dashboard of my heart have turned back off, I'm ready for the blinking cursor on my screen.

When people in my industry ask how I manage my workload, I tell them it's by strategically opening the release valves with extreme sports. After watching Wayne Cordero's "Dead Leader Running" talk multiple times, I now build my year around these beneficial encounters with fear. I schedule a beautiful adventure or a notable adrenaline rush right before and then right after my two perennial busy seasons.

That's what led me to Mason Wing Walking Academy a few weeks before my autumn gauntlet of job orders. I took their introductory and intermediate courses in wing walking on a 1943 Boeing Stearman. After several hours of training and practice, we headed out over the Strait of Juan de Fuca that separates the Olympic Peninsula from British Columbia's Vancouver Island. I rode in the cockpit in front of Keith, a retired Air Force pilot and the man responsible for pulling a dozen aerobatic maneuvers while I was out on the wings.

I had watched all six of my classmates fly from our grass strip and then land there again. In between, I had watched the plane pirouette against a blue ceiling. We heard the 450-horsepower engine scream and then go silent, as the fabric-covered biplane soared up into a loop or fell from a stall. That wood-framed aircraft delivered other pupils with arms raised and fists pumping.

During a lull in our private air show, I debriefed Erin, a classmate who had just returned from her flight.

"What are you feeling right now?"

The travel nurse paused, looked out into the sky from which she'd just arrived, and answered, "An incredible peace." Her answer, though maybe surprising to some, matched the joy and satisfaction on her face. Contentment glowed in her eyes. Accomplishment straightened her shoulders. She took deep breaths to archive the air and the aura that enveloped us students.

When I landed an hour or so later, I knew what Erin meant. Before I even exited the cockpit, I yelled, "I've never been more alive!" I had relinquished my fears to Keith's talent, to the harnesses' security, to the plane's reliability, and to the laws of physics. Those concessions produced something in me that transformed me into a walking exclamation mark—an exclamation mark in the thickest possible font. That surrender earned a reward of exclusive, indescribable sensations.

When most of us hear the word *peace*, we usually picture a quiet calm, a tranquil place, a smiling exhale. If peace were an image, you're probably picturing morning mist rising off a secluded pond, a field of wildflowers and butterflies, or a beach all to yourself at sunset. Erin didn't misuse that word, though. Peace can also feel like a thumping relief along a ragged seam where the warring has just stopped. She, my fellow students, and I had just witnessed the battle between our fears and our faith. We saw it end in real time. That ceasefire wafted like catharsis, raining on the smoldering rubble of new territory we had captured for our legacy.

I've encountered that same sensation after a trembling obedience to a Holy Spirit assignment. I've felt that relief when relinquishing my plans and adapting them to Heaven's prompting. My lungs have pumped out a similar exhale after a scary surrender to Jesus. My throat has offered a similarly cracked exclamation after seeing God work through my compliance with the guiding principles of Scripture. I've felt that renewed, awakened peace—not because of avoidance of challenges and fears but because of fighting and winning battles over them.

On the days I've resisted arrogance with all the ammo I've been given, I sleep better. When I've raged against my greed by making a generous leap, I don't need to veg on my phone to escape stress. When I've noticed my insecurity triggered but have behaved instead out of truth, I exhale like Erin did. My shoulders release.

But before the after-party comes the tension. Before the "Woot!" my knees shake. I rub my hands down dry pant legs. I need to use the bathroom—and then again five minutes later. Before Jesus shows off his creative flow, it's common for my fitness tracker to show my beats per minute jumping higher. But because God wired me for adventure, he knows I'll thank him later.

I recently took my little friend, Raelyn, for a ride in my MINI. She'd been wanting to ride in "Mr. Ryan's race car" for weeks. All buckled in, we turned a hot lap of our church's parking lot and broke into some emergency brake slides out in an adjacent field. When I delivered her back to her mom, Raelyn declared that it was a "little fun" but that she was "a little scared." Her mom and I looked at her and then at each other. We could tell she meant "a lot" instead of "a little." I felt so bad!

By Raelyn's definition, I've been "a little scared" too many times to count—on purpose. For your sake, I hope you have too. I hope you have many moments of feeling "a little scared" ahead of you, and I hope you someday have a book's worth of stories of how God brought you indescribable joy and a welcome peace.

SCARED OF HEIGHTS

Fear can be a catalyst or an excuse.

When you're homeschooled, it's really easy to get a consensus on where to take your senior trip. My brother and I both wanted to go to New Zealand for his. For some reason, my parents agreed to the deal. They even signed over temporary custody of my brother, so I could sign for all his release forms. In return, I offered to go first on every adrenaline rush. That way, if they lost a son, it would be their weird one.

I remember the first thing we tried: wire-guided BASE jumping off the sixty-third story of Sky Tower in Auckland. At that point in my life, the highest thing I'd ever jumped off was a playground swing. But there I was, looking down at tiny cars on Victoria Street below and cargo ships in the harbor that looked small enough to be Battleship game pieces. My legs felt like concrete when I tried to move them closer to the edge of the jump platform. When I admitted that later to Timmy, he replied, "Yeah. You looked constipated."

A few days later, we went for a scarier leap. We took a tiny, open-air cable car with a metal-grate floor out to a swaying bungee jump station that hung in the middle of Nevis Canyon—440 feet above the Shotover River. The glass-walled room included a floor with a strip of glass in it so you could watch the jumpers in front of you. We jumped in descending order from heaviest to lightest. When my turn came, I waddled out to the diving board feeling even more vulnerable with my ankles cinched together. Block, the jump master, asked if I was alright. "I'm scared," I answered.

"That's good, mate," Block replied. "The more scared you are now, the better the ride will be." He then explained that working there every day had taken the rush out of it for him. He needed to climb on the outside of the hanging jump station and leap off the top to get a little buzz from the jump.

A few seconds later, Block counted down. *Three! Two! One!* And then I obediently leaned forward and fell into a 400-foot swan dive.

If you jump at a first-rate bungee operator, you're attached in a full-body harness—not just around your ankles. To keep blood from rushing to your head, you get a second opportunity for faith. At the height of your third rebound, you have to reach for your ankles and pull a pin that releases your feet from the harness. On the fourth time down, you drop into a seated position and wait to be winched back to the platform. It makes total sense when they explain it before your jump and as I type it now. At the moment, though—hanging upside down—it feels odd to look up at the only thing connecting you to safety and pulling a pin. You do it, though, because someone who knows better told you that's the best way. Turns out, it's way easier to do before you run out of those weightless moments.

When I tell people stories like this, one of the most common replies they give is, "I could never do that. I'm scared of heights."

They always seem unprepared when I return their excuse with, "So am I."

See, I jump *because* it scares me.

If that doesn't make sense to you, think about what Block told me. "That's good, mate. The more scared you are now, the better the ride will be." See, our sympathetic nervous system dumps chemicals into our bloodstream at fight-or-flight moments. I'm not sure if that release is proportional to the fear, but I can report that Block was right about fear producing adrenaline.

You know this to be true. The first time you drove a car, your hands probably sweated. You might have taken a big breath before pulling out onto that first road. You definitely held on with both hands. Now, you can scroll through podcast options while driving seventy miles per hour on the highway and not even blink. The first time you rode a roller coaster, you held on for dear life. By the fifth time, you could pose for goofy pictures when the flash popped. Your body was still dropping down that big hill with the same sensations, but your brain reminded you, "This ends well." Think about the difference in heart rate between your first day of a dating relationship or college or your current job. Your Fitbit readings would be significantly different than those on your fourth date, your fifth week of college, or this past Monday at your work.

I was explaining all of this for the hundredth time a few weeks ago at a gathering of advertising professionals. One of them interjected, "You realize you're talking about this in terms that an addict would use?"

I laughed. The idea of an adrenaline junkie hails from almost thirty years ago, and I've been cognizant of the potentially dangerous reality in my own life for a solid decade of that span. That's why I've intentionally avoided picking one adrenaline rush and diving deep into it. To get that same wave of epinephrine and norepinephrine, junkies must try bigger and scarier stunts. They have to push the envelope further and further to enjoy the same hormonal release that proceeds the dopamine reward. That's why BASE jumpers and wingsuit athletes have such a high mortality rate. Too often, when you spend time at the edge, you find it.

While I often feel most alive when I'm scared, I like staying well within the border of where my life would be in danger. So, I take a different approach than a singularly focused addict. I try a bunch of different things that elevate my heart rate and make my knees weak. I get that same adrenaline dump but from within the relative safety of introductory experiences.

I still get scared doing tourist-level adventures. For example, I used to bring friends and family up to Maryland's Eastern Shore for hang gliding lessons. It was my jam for half a decade, and I recruited groups as large as 17 people at a time from my church to join me. The last time I went up there—not the first time but the *last* time—my legs were shaking as the tow plane pulled us up to release height. My instructor, hanging in the sleeve below me, could feel the vibration. About 2,000 feet off the hard deck, he assured me, "We'll slow down when we unhook. It won't be as cold."

"I'm not cold," I replied.

"Oh."

People tell me all the time that they couldn't hang glide or bungee jump or skydive because they would be "too scared." I'm not sure where the line is between appropriately scared and too scared, but life gets better when we're at least a little scared. Almost all of our greatest accomplishments were and are birthed in fear. If you're married, you took a big chance and probably a big breath on your wedding day. If you're working at a job that gives you more than just a paycheck, you risked something when applying. If you and your partner made a baby, you tipped over the first in a winding line of hundreds of adventure dominoes. If you left home for opportunities far from home, you did the same thing I do all over the planet. You looked fear and uncertainty dead in the eyes and proceeded anyway. You went from *I've never* or *I couldn't* to *I just did.*

In adrenaline rushes from action sports, that line between "haven't yet" and "now you're doing it" can be as short as a half second and clearly marked. Your kayak teeters off the rock into the rain-swollen creek. Your heels leave the edge of the bridge or airplane. The stoplight goes green. Your front tire hits the jump. But the same holds true of other moments: when you hit *Send* on that text or that phone number, when you step up to a microphone, when you drop a letter into the metal slot at the post office. I feel that "well here we go" sensation pulse immediately after someone asks me a question about my beliefs, my motives, or my behavior. You probably have your own list of watershed moments like that—big and small.

In some (if not most) of these situations, you were rewarded for your bravery. In all of them, you grew. You learned something and gained confidence for the next adventure. You trained your brain that this sensation was good. Even if you're not an adrenaline junkie, you've absorbed the equivalent of the gateway drugs.

When my friends and teammates ask me to pray courage over a challenge they face, I ask Jesus to reward their obedience. "Let them feel your presence and pleasure so much that they crave more of it—that it'll be habit forming." Just as with whitewater kayaking or paragliding, I'm not sure if the ensuing euphoria is proportional to the faith required in spiritual obedience; but it sure feels that way. Jesus designed us with dopamine, oxytocin, serotonin, and endorphins. He's certainly not opposed to lavishing any or all of them on us. He lived in that reality too. Whoever wrote the book of Hebrews said that Jesus endured a horrific, sacrificial obedience "for the joy set before him."

The junkie is not always dominant in me. When it is, though, I do things in part *because* I'm afraid. My fingers tremble. My deodorant fails. My heart accelerates. Apparently, I look constipated? You get the idea.

After the jump, I shout and dance. After the rapids, I yell and pump my fist. After the difficult spiritual conversation, I thank Jesus from my knees or from the driver's seat on a scenic drive. There's a catharsis, a reset. I feel connected to eternity. At times when I've been a conduit for Jesus' grace, electricity seems to pulse in my veins. And just like when a group of us take on a physical adventure, when someone in my circle of faith performs a spiritual act of bravery or stout act of obedience, a collective energy radiates back and forth between us. It's joy. It's celebration. It's all something we wouldn't have if fear wasn't conquered.

What I'm saying is, leaning into your fear is worth it.

For the record, I'm not toying with venomous snakes, playing chicken with an oncoming train, or opening the emergency exit on commercial flights. Please hear me: I'm not advocating a death wish. Don't go stand in the middle of the interstate and ask Jesus to reveal himself. He will answer that but differently than you're hoping. At the same time, the way of Jesus is often not safe. While he tells us over and again not to fear, he keeps putting those he loves in places that reasonably cause fear. Personally, I think that's by design. We don't need faith in Jesus when we're comfortable. We don't need to trust his sovereignty when everything's just a religious ritual. As long as we are in a relationship with an infinite being, there will be questions and doubt, discomfort and uncertainty.

Something tells me the reward for faith-led obedience in our next life—even if we don't feel rewarded in our current one—will make us glad we embraced the unknown in the here and now. If we knew now what we'll know then, we'd probably be running toward more of our fears instead of letting them push us away. If we saw the heights of glory that await us, we might embrace more of the heights we fear down here.

THE TALENT

"You don't have to go fast."

My personal best for top speed in a parking garage is 37 miles per hour. I know it's not some kind of a record, though, because Daijiro Yoshihara blew my doors off in the same parking garage on the same day. In fact, he was paid to do it. The 2011 Formula DRIFT world champion was my stunt double for a car commercial.

Several months earlier, I had entered a contest. After MINI had released a new Cooper model in Europe with a bulldog-themed campaign, MINI USA decided to launch a series of ads with a more American feel. They knew the biggest pushback to the new, larger Cooper would be from MINI enthusiasts who like their MINIs—well—mini. Since those who drive these cars tend to be the brand's best salespeople, current MINI owners were asked to submit ideas on how we'd test the new model.

More than 800 of us submitted ideas, which the marketing team sifted down to 20. They posted them online for public vote, promising to make a commercial out of the one that received the most likes. My MINI buddies, Brian and Michelle, won that contest; but MINI USA ended up making commercials out of their marketing team's favorite ten.

My concept made the cut.

Kind of.

My original idea was for a chase scene in a parking garage. I would speed up and around each level to the roof, where I'd bolt out of the hatchback, run over to the edge of the parking deck, and jump onto the strut of a waiting helicopter. The ad agency loved it, but we couldn't get it past the various legal teams. I offered to sign any indemnity waiver that came with an airbag below, but they had to rewrite the script. The final concept was for a guy (me!) to see how fast he could drive from the entrance up to the roof deck and back down.

The marketing folks scouted parking garages via Google Maps until they found one in downtown Los Angeles. The final choice held a tight-spiral exit ramp in the middle of the structure surrounded by decks that rose around it. To add a degree of showmanship and demonstrate the new MINI Cooper's backup camera, the hero would drive down the spiral backward.

You know: your average Saturday afternoon test drive.

The ad agency flew my wife and me out to Los Angeles, hired a limo to convey us to a beachfront hotel, gave us hundreds of dollars of walk-around money, and then sent an agency rep to drive us to the shoot. They made us feel like Hollywood had been waiting for our debut. We were blown away by the size of craft services (the catering spread) and the wardrobe RV. I was enamored with the chase camera vehicles, and I was stunned that it took a tractor trailer of equipment to film a ninety-second spot. The call sheet listed just short of seventy people for various roles. One woman's job was just making sure my sleeves were pulled up to the same spot for every take, and that was an important detail because most of my scenes included only my hands.

See, I was driving the "show car." While Dai screeched tires up and down the garage, I was driving an identical vehicle. The cars held two significant differences. First, my car's passenger seat had been removed. In its place was bolted a $200,000 periscope camera. Its lens extended in front of my face and elbowed right off the end of my nose. Also, my car included a camera operator—who had just returned from shooting a Beyoncé video—riding in the back seat, watching a monitor, and recommending adjustments.

In a way, Dai and I were both rookies. He had never driven a MINI, and I had never been in a TV commercial. Everybody on the set knew he was the precision driver. After a few takes, almost everybody knew I was what the call sheet labeled "the talent." Strangely, though, only the few ad agency staffers seemed to know that I wasn't a paid actor. The production crew did not. For someone who screwed up the only two lines of his stage career, I found this unsettling. (Seriously: I botched "woof woof" and "bark bark" as Sherlock Holmes's dog in a fourth grade play.) While actors are paid for literally portraying what they're not, I felt like an imposter, a poser, one of those nervous conmen in a heist movie.

When the director yelled "Action!" my heart rate sped faster than the four pistons under the hood. *What!?* I thought. I didn't feel ready. I thought somebody would've given me more specific instructions, but they didn't know that I was clueless. For all they knew, I was a journeyman actor taking small jobs until I caught a break.

I hadn't practiced anything. I couldn't have. The vehicles were sequestered until shooting during a tight recording window. I just showed up willing to embrace whatever they asked.

The crew eventually learned of my amateur status not only from the number of takes but also from all the questions I asked. They seemed amused by my curiosity and surprised by my interest in their careers. They returned my inquiries with humility and patience and thorough explanations. I learned *so much* that day. People make fun of actors and actresses on late-night shows that gush about a costar's generosity. That word—generosity—makes sense to me, though, after six hours with the film crew, ad agency folks, and MINI USA's marketing brass. It felt like they were rooting for me, that they wanted me to have fun. Just watching them do their job was entertaining and intriguing to me. Being authentic about that wonder seemed to spark a little joy in their Saturday afternoon overtime.

Maybe that's why they let me try to film a scene meant for Dai. At the forty-second mark of the commercial, the racer pulls an emergency brake slide, flips from forward into reverse, and then backs into the spiral ramp. We had a few minutes to blow before lunch, and Dai was busy sliding around corners downstairs. The film crew let me know I didn't have to drive fast. "We can speed it up in post. Just focus on smooth movement."

The problem was that the curb was ridiculously tall. Oh, and at the start of the ramp, the radius of the spiral proved irregular. I couldn't make the take long enough or smooth enough for them to use despite four attempts. I fell well short of impressing Rich Rutherford, our stunt coordinator and one of Hollywood's most notable precision drivers.

While Rich let me know my mistakes came with my beginner

territory, the film crew got on the radio. "Hey, Dai, can you come up to the roof for a quick shot before lunch?" A few minutes later, the nonchalant wünderdriver jumped into my car and pulled off the high-speed reverse launch. On his first take. I would've been more embarrassed had I not been so impressed with what I'd just watched.

I stood on that concrete rooftop only for an hour at most, but I can remember it like yesterday. The same holds true of different rooftop moments along my faith journey. On multiple occasions, I've stood back and watched Jesus do something amazing in contrast to my meager contributions. Jesus humbly lets me know he's better at sovereignty than I am—better at intervention and healing too. Like Rich, he doesn't make me feel less-than for my ignorance, inexperience, and incompetence. Jesus demonstrates his strength through my weakness, his mastery through my mistakes.

On the night before I wrote this chapter, several of my buddies and I discussed how long God waited for Noah to build his ark. The Speaker of the universe could've made a boat of any size instantly appear. He was open to supernatural intervention because he brought animals to Noah and caused them to chill out for a few months. Also, there's that whole global flood thing. For some reason, though, Noah was assigned to roughly a hundred years of public manual labor.

And God waited.

"You don't have to go fast. We can speed it up in post."

Apparently, there was something for Noah to learn in the process. Maybe Jesus wanted to give the spectating world more time to reconsider their rejection. Maybe the Holy Spirit wanted to give them extra doses of Noah's faithfulness to absorb.

Going strictly on the ancient Hebrew narrative, Noah wasn't introduced as a professional shipbuilder or even any kind of builder.

What qualified him for his assignment wasn't a profession or a paycheck. He didn't have to make a pretty boat. This wasn't a Royal Caribbean ship with zip lines and rock climbing walls. Heaven's voice gave him some dimensions, some material specifications, and some time to figure it out. "When you're done, gather your family, some animals, and food. And. Action!"

I can just hear Noah exclaiming, "Wait. What!?"

In our self-made-success America, it's tempting to think we need to start our own 501C3 charity to change the world or that we have to get a paycheck from a church to be a shepherd of souls. Don't you have to go to seminary first to explain the Bible to friends?

No. You don't even need Lori Loughlin or Felicity Huffman to help you fake a seminary degree.

Jesus said he chooses unqualified people on purpose—so that we can't take credit for his supernatural results. That means you're just as likely to get an assignment from him where you have no expertise as you are a task that leverages your trained skills. The Director wants us to show up and be willing to follow his instructions. He welcomes our questions. He smiles on our humility. If your experience is anything like mine, he'll even give you multiple takes sometimes—several chances to get it right.

We don't need to be embarrassed by our inexperience. We don't have to hide our naivety or nervousness. Jesus gives us crazy opportunities to represent him, but he recruits novices. Heaven's film crew doesn't snicker when we lurch out of first gear. Our "great cloud of witnesses" is cheering for us, rooting for us.

For sure, Jesus uses professional ministers every day of every week. If you serve in vocational ministry, you are making beautiful art—even if you contribute only the equivalent of the best avocado wrap a camera operator has ever tasted. If your job is just helping people pull up their sleeves for the work, fold those cuffs like Heidi Klum will be inspecting them. You have the opportunity to help us nonprofessionals see the big picture and chase big dreams.

For the rest of us—for those of us who feel underqualified or at least uncomfortable in our assignment—know that Jesus chose us for our roles. He's not embarrassed by our mistakes. He's sovereign. If our flubs were going to be too much for his reputation, he could go back in time and keep George and Lorraine McFly from getting together. What I mean is that he could head us off well before the pass.

We don't have to end injustice overnight. We don't need to finish our ark by next Sunday. We aren't asked to back our cars up like we stole them. We just have to be in our assigned place and ready for Jesus to call, "Action!"

INDIRECTV

How to shake retention specialists and your own regret.

My parents got rid of the television in our house when I was four years old. Five years later, my grandma bought us a new TV, and my sisters and I spent the next several years making up for lost time. Before the days of DVRs and streaming video, I binged on reruns and after-school cartoons. My concerned dad contested all of this. He regularly remarked how TV was corrupting my mind and that I should be outside more. He wasn't wrong. I'd have been better off with more drawing with my Prismacolor pencils, more BMX riding and jumping, more innings of Wiffle ball, and maybe even more of those board game marathons.

A decade later at my private college, we couldn't have TVs or Internet in our dorm rooms; and the community TV on each floor came alive only for the evening news, the World Series, the Super Bowl, and the NBA Finals. I followed my teams via radio news updates and through the Monday edition of *USA Today* in the campus bookstore. When I was home from college, I worked two jobs or served as a camp counselor. I didn't really have time for TV.

That didn't change much after college, either. I got married four months after graduation and spent that first year of marriage making memories in a new town with my wife. I spent the evenings pecking out chapters of my first book, swimming laps, and playing water basketball at our YMCA. Then, on the Tuesday after our first anniversary, the September 11 terrorist attacks played out on the TV in the break room at my work. That night, Crystal and I bought our first TV. We quickly signed up for cable channels—one of the first times in my life I'd seen them outside of an airport.

Just as I did in my middle school years, I started making up for lost time on our 11-inch TV. I watched VH1's *I Love the 90s* series to learn what I had missed in pop culture. I got hooked on *Survivor* and other "reality" shows. I even applied to be on two competition shows and actually became an alternate on a Discovery Channel pilot, where contestants competed in physics experiments while riding coasters at Six Flags. Crystal and I practically mainlined *Trading Spaces* and *Newlyweds*. I lounged on the couch through marathons of *Junkyard Wars* and found myself watching up to 10 hours of NFL programming on Sundays.

Several years after diving into this chronic binging, we transitioned from our Spanish-speaking church to the English-speaking one we now attend. Our new pastors held backgrounds in rock climbing, backpacking, ice climbing, whitewater rafting, and racing motorcycles. Over time I made friends with guys from church who flew ultralights and powered parachutes. My new friends invited me to try whitewater rivers in their canoes and kayaks; others invited me on international backpacking trips. I played pickup basketball with our church staff three mornings a week. A group of my friends started doing nocturnal hikes on full moon Friday nights in the winter. Eventually, I was serving with my buddies in our church's parking lots two or three services a weekend and setting out the cones and signs on Saturdays. Throughout all of this, I was engaging in Bible studies and community prayer experiences one or two nights a week or on Saturday mornings.

And then one day I asked Crystal, "Babe, when was the last time you had the TV on?" (She had won us a 42" flat screen in a drawing.)

"The Grammys, I think?"

For me, it had been the Super Bowl.

It was now April.

So, I called DirecTV to cancel our service. As you know, cable and satellite companies offer you all kinds of incentives to keep your subscription. "Maybe you need more channels," my retention representative offered. "Maybe you're not watching TV because you don't have the channels that interest you." Not a bad theory or attempt, but I told him we'd had the TV on only twice that year.

"Why aren't you watching TV?" he asked in amazement. He followed with something like, "What are you doing with your time?"

I remember the exact words of my answer to this day: "I'm blogging, whitewater kayaking, and having meaningful conversations with my friends."

"Wow. You're living the life," he replied. "Good for you, man. I'll tell you what. I'm going to put a note on your account for them not to reach out to you." He added something about us not being satellite TV candidates.

After I hung up, I thought back to how much my dad would've celebrated this three decades earlier. Between you and me, part of me wishes that TV had gotten crowded out of my life sooner too. I'm not saying TV is inherently bad. This wasn't a moral decision about content. We still go to movies on date nights or with groups of friends. Crystal now shares a Netflix account with some girlfriends, and she has a few series she follows. I'll jump in on the couch with her from time to time, and I'll catch a small handful of football games each season on my phone.

No, what I wish had come sooner was the displacement. I wish more of those enriching moments had crowded out the binging and the mindless hours. I wish I had moved earlier from spectator to participant. Instead of living vicariously through actors, athletes, and contestants, I now get regular chances to be a character or even the protagonist in real-life adventures. That goes for both physical exploits and spiritual encounters. I've had the opportunity to marvel at God's creation and observe Jesus making himself known in my heart and the hearts of my friends. I've had moments where I've felt truly alive and connected to eternity.

It's been several years since we canceled satellite service, and the DirecTV dish is still perched on the roof above our bathroom. It stands out to me sometimes when I pull in the driveway. It's an altar of sorts—a reminder of a season of my life. I'm still tempted to waste time as a spectator. Facebook, Instagram, and sometimes Twitter prove my new drugs of choice. But now I know the path out of those habits. The only way to replace wasted time is to fill that space with an activity or relationship that I love more than scrolling on social media.

I've turned off audible and visual notifications on my phone so that I can be more present in those life-giving activities. With resources from wise people and some journaling, I've learned how to incentivize participation in kingdom activities and relationship-building, even though they aren't as easy as couch time in front of a glowing screen.

To help with that, I've embraced the concept of spiritual pathways—think of them as love languages for your relationship with Jesus. We humans feel most connected to our Creator when operating in one or more of several relational channels. (Depending on which resource you read, there are seven to nine different lanes.) I take the test every few years, as my scores change a touch. For more than a decade, though, nature is the primary pathway where I've felt closest to Jesus.

Multiple days a week, I spend at least an hour alone with Jesus outdoors. At least once a week, I'll take my laptop or journal to a solitary place to process my circumstances and unburden my soul. And several times a year, I seek out places that make me feel small—that remind my wayward soul of the size of both my accomplishments and my problems.

To enhance the outdoor experience I listen to music with lyrics about faith and surrender, acceptance and holiness, humility and praise. That music hushes my world, settles my heart, and fills me with resolve. So, instead of chanting to myself not to do or say or feel something detrimental—or actually doing the malignant behavior—I just go do something proven to distract my mind or move my heart toward a good thing that replaces it. I might take a hike with headphones playing a worship playlist. Or I'll stand next to a river or, better yet, paddle a kayak on one and listen for its inherent soundtrack. On the weekend, I sometimes drive winding mountain roads and look out over pastures and forests. Before or after shifts in the office, I regularly take an exaggerated inhale and exhale while watching a sunrise or sunset.

These are some of the regular practices I use to center my soul.

Your list might include tending flowerbeds or painting or marching in a protest for justice. You might recenter your soul by serving at a homeless shelter, in a mentoring session, or on a mission trip. You might realign the spine of your life with the chiropractic care of reading theology books or journaling or listening to podcasts from far-flung churches. You might settle your heart with the innocence of reading storybooks to your nieces and nephews or giggling with your grandkids. Several of my friends have been reduced to tears when they encounter Jesus in a prayer labyrinth. Others of my friends feel connected to the Eternal when jumping up and down with middle schoolers at a summer camp.

Wherever you find Jesus, go there.

Whatever brings you closer to him, so you sense his presence and prompting, do that.

Then do more of it.

The Apostle Paul wrote that we should set our minds on the good and wholesome things Jesus has placed in our world. He knew that minds occupied with those gratitude-laced thoughts will displace doubt and selfishness and apathy. He knew what makes us feel eternally alive would combat the evil and death of our fallen world. Paul also taught his readers to be filled with the Holy Spirit so that we wouldn't behave in ways that grieve Jesus. If our hearts and thoughts and calendars are filled with goodness, we have a lot less room to entertain temptation. If we add moments of positive eternal impact, we won't need as much space to store regret.

Or episodes on the DVR.

LIFE INSURANCE

Bungee jumping into "one another"

It took me seemingly forever to get life insurance. Crystal and I were married at least a dozen years before a motivated insurance agent found a policy that didn't ask the standard ten questions about what underwriters consider risky behavior. Even though I have high cholesterol, most actuaries seemed more concerned that I've jumped out of planes and racked up some speeding tickets. I remember the last attempt with the standard ten questions. With some pride and definitely amusement, I answered, "I've done eight of those, and this summer I'll be doing number nine."

The only one on the list that has never applied to me is riding motorcycles. I've driven them on farms and Peruvian back roads but never on an American street. I'm not allowed. I made this sweet deal with my wife. Crystal told me I could do all of the other nine activities (and more) as long as I didn't own a motorcycle. So, if you're scoring at home: I'm allowed to jump off buildings and out of airplanes. I have her permission to climb mountains and whitewater kayak. She condones rock climbing and hang gliding. She kisses me before I leave to paraglide and race my car at the track. All I had to give up is owning a motorcycle.

Crystal's rationale is sound too. She explained it to me this way, "When you do those other things, you're always with a professional or an expert. If you had a motorcycle, you'd be doing it by yourself. I trust the professional. I just don't trust you." Before you think that sounds harsh, know that I full-heartedly agree with her. In fact, I get the most nervous on the activities that give me the most autonomy. The more I have control over an adventure, the higher my heart rate. I'm clumsy and irrational. I regularly forget important steps. I've not developed the muscle memory or the counterintuitive instincts most adventure sports require. I make mistakes. I prove my wife right over and over again.

So, with this logic in place, you might be surprised how I predicted my death.

Three years before our friend Jen stood in our wedding, she wrote my obituary. Don't judge her. I wrote hers too. We shared a former Associated Press writer as our instructor for Intro to Journalism. It was 1997, and Ms. Green warned us that most newspaper writers worked their way up the ladder starting from the obituary section. If we wanted to see our names someday on front-page bylines, we would need to get noticed from how we described finished lives. So, she paired us with a classmate; and we interviewed each other about the life we forecasted for ourselves. Then, we had to craft and edit those stories into something interesting. I gave Jen an interesting ending, and she had to make do with the rest. My demise took seconds. My bungee cord snapped during a bridge jump.

I died doing something that the college-sophomore version of me assumed I would someday love. What I didn't realize was how unlikely that death would have to be.

A decade later, I bungee jumped for the first time out of a New Zealand cable car. The jump rig held something like 27 international engineering patents. Everything was checked and rechecked before every jump. As I've experienced every time I've jumped, my exact weight was written on my hand with a Sharpie and called out multiple times over radios and intercoms before each jump to make sure I was attached to the weight-appropriate bungee. See, bungee lines come in different thicknesses so that people of various weight ranges can all fall to similar depths. Weight-specific lines also minimize the strain on the bungees. At a bridge jump in South Africa, I learned that bungee jump lines are rated to be reliable for up to 900 jumps. That vendor retired bungees after 300 to 500 jumps. They recovered the costs of those early retirements by cutting the cords into eight-inch sections and selling them to euphoric and nostalgic customers like me.

I've held that eight-inch section of the cord in my hand multiple times, and it always feels weird—like I'm physically holding a secret. Tourist bungee jumpers never get to feel their bungee. It's typically wrapped in a nylon sleeve that is attached to your harness by a professional. So, you have to trust what's in there is good enough. When I show friends the sample, I point out the cross section. A jump station bungee isn't one simple cord but more than a hundred rubber strands bound together by outer strands. No single one of those strands could support my weight. Heck, no twenty of them could. With their proximity and surface tension, though, lots of independently weak cords work in unison to hold my weight through a tremendous stretch. The thicker cords for heavier customers like me don't contain thicker strands—just more strands.

In a moment of clarity from his rants, the author of Ecclesiastes recommended adding strands to our support cords. He noted that having a companion makes us safer and helps keep us warm, but having two people with us is even better. For emphasis he added, "Woe is he who has nobody to help them."

All of that probably seems obvious to most people. For those who've read this warning and thought it was unnecessary advice, I need to apologize. That's in there for people like me. If that's you too, you probably share my tendency to jump into something in life with just your one, little strand of strength. I fail to add strands to my endeavor.

I don't mind paying vendors to do things for me, but I struggle to ask for volunteer help. I've never asked someone to help me move. I'll grab an Uber to the airport before I'll ask someone—even sometimes my wife—to drive me there. I pay my friends or barter to help me with car repairs—and only ask them when I've exhausted my other paid options. Nobody other than a lawn service has ever cut my grass while I'm on vacation. I don't ask for favors or discounts.

I hate asking for help.

I'm not bragging. That doesn't make me a better person. If anything, it makes me weaker. In those moments when the illusion of self-sufficiency unravels, I realize how unsafe it is to be alone. My strand starts to crack. The strain causes me to fray. When the weight of life increases, I feel it stealing my elasticity. When demands and dysfunction grow heavy, I get frustrated at my frailty. For the record, that frustration is a good thing in the same way a warning light on your dashboard is a good thing. Those orange or red indicators appear before we do irreparable damage. They let us know that something isn't right before we are faced with expensive or catastrophic failure.

Through nature or nurture, some of us are thicker strands; but none of us are complete bungee cords. Nobody is a super strand. That's why we need fellow strands. Even God exists in multiple strands. Before there was Earth or anything on it, Jesus, the Father, and the Holy Spirit agreed: "Let us make mankind in our image." A force with the power to speak unfathomable life into existence didn't do it alone. The sovereignty that instantaneously created incomprehensible complexity out of thin air, asked for help.

"Let us."

Let's do this together.

Jesus knows about my life what my wife knows about my adventures: I'm safer with others. Community and accountability are features—not bugs—of his system. He wants us to ask for help. While he welcomes those requests to come his way, he saturated the New Testament with commands to ask others too. He calls us to symbiotic relationships with fellow journeyers. He didn't command us necessarily to have friends—to chase friendship as an end in itself. Instead, he asked us to demonstrate actions and characteristics of true friendship to co-laborers of his harvest.

When we do this with and for each other, we build something that is bigger than us, something that outlives us. Like a bungee cord, we become more effective because of the sum of the parts. We gain a collective elastic ability to help people rebound, to enable impressive feats, to keep sporadic burdens from leading to someone's demise.

All of this requires more than liking someone or sharing interests with them. This kind of community requires surface tension from lives rubbing up against each other. This symbiotic support begins when we ask other strands to pray with us or for us. This camaraderie grows as we ask other strands for counsel and forgiveness. Brotherhood and sisterhood blossom when we ask our friends for context, for reminders, and for Scripture. Accountability flowers when we ask them to check in on us.

These are requests I'm still learning to make—awkwardly and imperfectly. Man, am I thankful for the times I have, though! This safety line has held me when I wanted out of my ministry and wanted more out of my marriage. This stout cord has buoyed my career at multiple crossroads. This interwoven community has asked me hard questions and even called me stupid. (They were right.) They also affirmed the tiny green sprigs budding in me that needed freedom to grow.

One new thing that Jesus is doing for me in this area is revealing that he weaves the bungee cord better than I do. These other strands haven't always been people who share my pastimes. They haven't always held personalities to which I naturally gravitate. As with Jesus, I've found friends in unexpected places. Usually, they've appeared when I'm serving on a volunteer team on a shared mission. The Holy Spirit weaves more strands into that cord when I give folks the benefit of the doubt and endure awkward moments. I've built community and accountability by being vulnerable with both long-time friends and relative strangers who responded to that trust with their own.

I have to warn you. A good number of these support strands stayed in my life for only a season of weeks, months, or short years. We got our 300 or 500 jumps together and then got repurposed to our next missions. I'm thankful for Facebook keeping their new adventures in my view, even if now from a distance; but I've had more bittersweet, commissioning goodbyes than I care to count.

Almost everybody wants friends. We don't have to be told to value friendship. The challenge for many of us is to be a friend, a co-conspirator—a support strand. That level of friendship requires a two-fold vulnerability of allowing people to know the rough texture of our lives and to offer ourselves to hold firm when they are stretched. It's made weirder by the fact that it's not often the cool kids or the rich kids God assigns to us. I'm convinced that many of my support strands think I'm an odd duck.

If you want a thicker bungee, then dive into serving. If you want to meet people that share your heart, devote yourself to a heavenly cause, an eternal mission. If you want to feel other strands, wrap your arms around the lonely, the hurting, and the disenfranchised. If you want to be known and accepted at the soul level, you might have to give up your motorcycle and look for other adventures. If you want to see Jesus through your friends, y'all might have to jump into the unknown together.

You'll know you're there when everyone is holding onto each other.

IF YOU CAN HEAR ME

Do the next thing you know to do.

Just about every year since 2007, I've celebrated my birthday with my buddy, Jack. It's his birthday too. We were born on the twelfth day of the same month, twelve years apart. We both love the mountains to which we've emigrated, and we both regularly schedule outdoor escapes to let our souls exhale. For our birthday weekend trips, we've scaled granite cliffs and explored cave labyrinths. We've hang glided, unhooking from our tow plane at a mile off the ground; and we've jumped out of an airplane from more than twice that height. We've traversed zip lines and via ferratas and several sections of the Appalachian Trail. We almost always bring a third person, so that they can share in what Jack has dubbed "our annual birthday adventure."

Several years ago, we brought Jack's daughter. He had promised Brittany to take her skydiving someday, and she was ready to cash in that rain check. While Jack and Brittany jumped tandem, I trained for my first Accelerated Free Fall (AFF) jump. Basically, it's the first solo jump toward a skydiving license. Instead of tumbling out of the plane with someone strapped to my back, two instructors jumped with me, holding onto handles sewn into my jumpsuit. Instead of a forty-five-minute ground school, my classes took more than six hours.

Between you and me, most of those additional hours were spent planning for unfortunate contingencies. Until that morning, I had no idea how many different ways a civilian skydiving jump could go wrong. We learned what to do if our main chute didn't deploy, if it deployed incorrectly, and if it got tangled. They taught us the three different ways both of our chutes could actually deploy at the same time and what to do for each of those scenarios. Finally, they gave us instructions specific to our drop zone—where to land, how to get set up to land there, and where not to fly while getting ready for our approach.

It was a lot to remember. I failed in the simulator several times before eventually passing. Approved to jump, I boarded a twin-engine plane with no back seats. Riding next to the Plexiglass door up to the jump altitude made my knees shake. One of my instructors placed her hand on my knee and assured me I would do great. Then the light above the door glowed green. My other instructor slid the door up into the ceiling. Our videographer crawled out and hung off the back of the plane. My male instructor perched himself on the edge of the opening and invited me to the ledge.

It was time for what's called the "hotel checkout." When ready, I would nod my head to my instructor inside the plane to check in. Then I'd nod my head to my outdoor instructor to check out. Then I would drop my shoulders and let go. All four of us would then tumble into the sky. This whole process is timed and has to take place in a handful of seconds. There can be no hesitation once we're all in the door.

That all happened as planned, and the videographer jumped off the wing a half-second early to catch our exit from the plane. My feet curled up as I plummeted toward Earth, belly-side-down. I needed some help with adjustments in my form, but I stayed fairly steady. I struggled to find the little hacky sack of a handle for my ripcord. Watching both the altimeter and my struggle, my instructor reached over and deployed my chute for me.

Parenthetically, the moment a parachute opens is unlike anything I've ever experienced. It's a startling yank, especially when you don't know it's coming. People who do it in action movies make it look way easier and smoother than it is. Anyway, once that chute opened, I was finally doing this thing on my own.

Kinda.

I had a two-way radio strapped to my chest. Theoretically, I was capable of two-way communication; but I was instructed to keep my hands in my steering toggles and just listen to the instructor on the other end. He was on the ground in the landing area, having been handed a piece of paper with my name and the stripe pattern of my parachute. Mine was orange-white-orange. (All reserve chutes are solid colors—usually white—so that people on the ground know what chute you're using.) Because the instructor can't make out faces a mile away, he uses that tiny cheat sheet in his hand to guide you home. For clarity, no two student jumpers with the same parachute stripe pattern jump out of the plane at the same time.

Well, that's how it's supposed to work. Somehow, two orange-white-orange chutes deployed from the same planeload. Because I went first,

I didn't see the other and didn't consider that as an explanation for what was about to happen.

My radio crackled. "Hi, Ryan! If you can hear me, pull on your left toggle." So, I pulled on my left toggle. It occurred to me that this form of two-way communication was smart. "Ryan, if you can hear me, pull your right toggle—your right toggle." I pulled the handle in my right hand, and my chute turned right. I think we went through this Simon Says game another round before I realized I was heading away from the airport toward the interstate with my back to the drop zone. I kept waiting for my next instructions, as the altimeter on my wrist showed dropping numbers. I figured the instructor knew I had plenty of time to get to the landing zone. In the meantime, my ground instructor had been trying to figure out why the chute he thought was me was not obeying his requests.

All of a sudden I heard, "Ryan! I'm so sorry. I had the wrong chute. I've got you now." He proceeded to get me turned around in a general direction toward the airport. I would not be able to land where originally planned because I had less than 3,000 feet of elevation left to use. I was under 1,000 feet when I flew over two of the things on the no-no list: the airport hangars and the Tarmac, especially since it was (1) asphalt and (2) active. Worse yet, I was heading toward two runways, one of which was hot. That means there was active plane traffic on it.

¡No bueno!

I pulled a hard left toggle and started flying between the runway and the taxiway. The ground was getting close. "Give me a little left toggle." I did. "A little more." I was now flying down the taxiway. I kept lightly tugging with my left arm until I was flying over the grass between the taxiway and the Tarmac.

"Both toggles hard now!"

I hesitated because a friend of mine had broken his back at another skydiving vendor, dumping his chute too soon. Also, I was a bit skeptical of the instruction after the past two minutes of elevated heart rate. I knew I had to dump at thirty feet. *Was this really thirty feet?* I didn't know, but I obeyed.

My shoes hit the grass right before my knees did. My chute crumpled behind me, almost touching the Tarmac. I was on the ground! My ground instructor yelled an apology, but I shook my head. "No, man! I just got a better story." We both laughed. There was a lot of relief in both our chests.

I was reminded that day of some valuable advice: when you don't know what's next, do what you know to do.

To be sure, this story was birthed out of a series of accidents and misunderstandings; but I should've maneuvered toward the big open field southwest of the airport. I should've followed that by executing the J pattern I was taught for landing, even when important voices in my ear said otherwise. I should've realized that some people have inarguable expertise but not enough proximity to guide my choices.

I'm a huge proponent of mentoring. I'm the product of welcomed discipleship, and I coach others through both spiritual formation and life challenges. So, I don't mean to imply that we should be independent vigilantes out in the world, making up our own rules for following Jesus. If you have access to a mentor or life coach, soak up their counsel. If you have the gift of a spiritual director or an older sibling in the faith, do consult their wisdom.

There's going to come a day, though, when you've got more than one good option on the table. You're going to bump into a situation where none of the choices are inherently wrong or harmful. You might have to choose between branch offices in Chicago or Seattle. You might have to select a child to adopt from an agency with 100 beautiful young souls. You might face a menu of multiple church small groups to join or several different international missions to give your vacation days.

Then what?

Then you do what you know to do. You steer to the big field east of the airport. You talk to Jesus—alone and with loved ones, maybe even on your knees or laying on the ground. You make space to hear from him in silence or in nature. You create room for his voice while journaling or absorbing media related to the topic at hand. You Google what the Bible has to say about that topic. You consult people who love Jesus more than they love you but who love you too.

And then you make the call and just be Jesus wherever that call takes you. Paul, the mentor for a bunch of first-century faith leaders, wrote that no matter what we do, we should do it for Jesus. So, whether you work in Denver or San Francisco, be Jesus in your workplace. Whether you go to Guatemala or Sierra Leone, focus on listening instead of snapping selfies. Whether you coach soccer or Tee-ball, demonstrate peace and patience. Whether you adopt a boy or a girl, show the unconditional love Jesus has shown on you. Whether you major in marketing or physical therapy, pursue excellence, integrity, and empathy. If two girls want you to take them to the same prom—well, you're on your own there. Jesus was single, and so was I all through high school.

So many times, analysis paralysis can keep us from adventures with Jesus. We're afraid to pass on the right option, the plan A that we assume Sovereignty had destined for us. We want to know we're in the right place at the right time. We think Jesus is sweating and pacing somewhere, exclaiming, "Pick B! Pick B! Pick B!" If the recorded words of Jesus don't speak to your dilemma, though, he's rooting for you to bring heaven to Earth. Be compassionate and merciful. Be diligent and honest. Be selfless and submissive. Be hope. Be light. Bring life.

When you don't know what to do, do what's always good to do.

Adventure happens as a result of wrong choices as often as it does from right choices. So, the objective isn't adventure. I'm not sure fulfillment or assuredness is the objective, either. Jesus asked us to follow him and then to represent him—not necessarily to feel anything, not to chase anything. When we obey his commands and move with his prompting, though, it's amazing how exciting life gets, how the right choices look in retrospect, and how fulfilling it is in the big grass field west of the airport.

THE CARRIE POLE

There are no accidents with Jesus—only collisions.

This is how old I am: when I took driver's ed in high school, at least one of our videos was still shown from reel-to-reel projectors. I had experience running those scary machines because my family didn't have a TV for five years, and we watched a good quantity of reel-to-reel movies borrowed from the library. That random knowledge helped this homeschooler get his public school classmates to laugh, because I knew how to quickly rewind and re-watch a scene. Particularly, we loved re-watching a wrinkled retiree fly from his golf cart during a collision shown in our "Myths About Alcohol" video. Oh my gosh. Hilarious! Hearing his class' unanimous laughter, our instructor bristled. "What's wrong with you people!?"

At the time, I thought that moment of being accepted and making people laugh was going to be my highlight of the course—the indelible moment, the story I'd tell the most. Two decades later, though, that anecdote fell to a distant second, when a stranger totaled her car while driving at me. Not at my car. At me. I'll explain why in a minute.

First, you have to know that since August of 2006, I've served on my church's parking lot greeter team. I can say without hyperbole that this team has changed my life and the lives of my friends. We've come to the team from a variety of motivations, but we've found unity in our mission. It's our job to give people an uncommon welcome. We hope to catalyze a chain reaction that'll culminate with a new surrender inside the building. An interesting concoction of misfits and the well-mannered, we comprise the outdoor worship team that sets up the indoor worship team for kingdom success. Like mail carriers, we serve regardless of weather; and we usually attend the service in our neon hats or the hat hair they create.

On the rainy morning in question, the asphalt grew shiny—reflecting gray instead of black. The concrete bases for the light poles absorbed the rain and darkened to the same color gray as the asphalt. As a result, it was hard to see the poles in our lot. Every week, as the start of the service gets closer, traffic typically picks up speed because of parishioners' urgency. The same held true that morning when a young woman saw me waving hello up by a curbside parking spot. Instead of driving first to my teammate's area and then to me, she cut a beeline straight to me. And into a light pole. Hard. She hit it dead center, and her Chevy Malibu bounced back as steam from her radiator burst into a small cloud. (I later told her I can't wait to watch the slow-motion replay in heaven someday.)

My friend and teammate, Will, ran to her window. A doctor by trade, he professionally asked the driver, "Are you okay?"

Carrie calmly replied, "I've been meaning to talk to you."

Unbeknownst to Will, Carrie had recently been in his house, talking to his wife, April, about her spiritual journey and her doubts. April had told Carrie, "You need to talk to my husband. Will has wrestled with a lot of the same questions you have." That was an understatement, though April knew that. Before Will encountered Jesus, he participated in public debates with pastors about matters of faith and science. Through a series of absolutely uncanny events, though, Will transformed from a proud skeptic to a humble believer.

Back to our rainy morning, cars were still streaming in behind the totaled Chevrolet. Those of us in reflective vests quickly pushed Carrie's car out of the way. Somebody called a tow truck, and Will led Carrie inside to our breakfast cafe. They talked for more than an hour. I'm not sure exactly what Carrie's journey with Jesus looked like for the next several months. What I do know is that she eventually joined our parking team and was the only woman on my service's squad for a while. On our blue jeans and Carhartts team, she holds the distinction of being the first on our team to welcome folks while wearing leopard print pumps. I wish you could've seen how effervescent Carrie glowed, greeting fellow parishioners on that asphalt!

Before Carrie moved back to Florida, we held a bittersweet prayer circle. She thanked us for our influence on her journey, and I reflected on the most memorable thing from my drivers ed course. Our cardigan-wearing instructor had repeatedly told us, "There are no accidents—only collisions." He felt as though all accidents could be avoided by following driving laws and preventative caution. That might be true. I don't know.

What I do know is that a collision with the supernatural seems better than a happy accident.

Sometimes, when I'm training a new teammate, I'll point to what we affectionately call "the Carrie pole" and tell them one of our team mottos: "There are no accidents with God—only collisions with his sovereignty." It's just one of the stories we tell and retell of what Jesus has done in our parking lots. I can also walk that rookie to the spot behind the cones where Chris surrendered his life to Jesus. I can take you to where a woman whose name I didn't yet know melted into my arms, crying while my teammates circled for prayer over her recent loss of her daughter. I've seen the tears of grown men fall on that asphalt as we lay hands on them. Every couple of years, one of our teammates will get baptized while wearing their reflective vest. At least two couples on the team overcame infidelity in their marriage and have served on the team together. While we rarely see vehicle collisions—thankfully—we see collisions with the supernatural all the time.

Over and again amidst our team or out in the parking lots, I've seen wild coincidences change the trajectory of someone's spiritual journey. I'm talking the kind of odds where even Lloyd Christmas wouldn't have asked, "So, you're saying there's a chance!?"

I wish I could remember them all, but here's a tiny example. For several years, our campus held Saturday night services. They attracted both attendees and volunteers more likely to arrive in a convertible or listen to Jimmy Buffet or walk into the building in flip-flops. People would regularly go out to dinner together afterward. Waving and directing traffic on those nights typically included as much stress as a poolside nap. Except for the night of February 20. Because half of our team had called out that night, I covered all of the positions on the far side of the building. The previous weekend's services had been canceled because of snow—the first time that had happened in at least a decade at our church. That shifted our sermon series back a week and bumped Will's talk to that night. Yes, that Will, the same Will.

Behind the stage side of the building, I could hear the opening song vibrating through the walls. For whatever reason, our Saturday night services experienced far fewer late arrivals than our Sunday ones did; so, we didn't stay as long on the asphalt. Back then, I attended those evening services; and I tried not to miss more than the first song. I waited for our point man's call on the radio that the road was clear. He called it after a single car entered the lot on the other side of the building. I stayed on the asphalt, waiting for it to circumnavigate our building to one of the open spaces in front of me.

An old Lexus pulled into an empty spot, and I noticed its California plates. As the driver closed her door, I tried to create a moment where she felt seen and noticed at a big church. I asked, "What part of California?"

"Santa Barbara," she answered.

Record scratch.

At that time in my career, after sixteen years as a marketing assistant in the auction industry, I had advertised thousands of auctions across forty-seven states. Up until the summer prior to this parking lot encounter, though, I had never advertised a single auction in California. A real estate auction one town over from Santa Barbara had changed all that. That auction took until the day before this winter interaction for the property to close—in part because the president of Bank of America had to sign off on the deal.

"No way!" I answered. "I just sold a house to Oprah yesterday in Montecito."

"Like—the real Oprah?" she asked.

I added some details to prove my claim was legitimate, and she clarified that she and her family were actually from Montecito.

"This is my first time visiting here," she announced.

"Well, I'm glad you're here!"

As I accompanied her on the sidewalk, I explained, "Tonight's speaker is part of our teaching team, but he isn't one of our pastors. He was an atheist and evolutionist who actually used to debate pastors." I tried to explain that his miraculous journey led to a unique perspective on the night's topic, but I don't know if it came out like I wanted. Having watched Will's journey as he went from being my parking teammate to my teacher, I connected with his talks in a special way. So, I've typically erred on the side of hype.

Thankfully, the visiting Californian also connected with Will's talk. After the service, she slipped down front to talk to Will. I saw them pray together—I assume about what God was stirring in her because of his message. She walked out with tears flowing down her cheeks, having done business with God. She happened to walk past me; and I blurted, "It was good to have you here with us tonight!"

That was an understatement for me. I don't remember Will's topic that night. I do remember that God used a blizzard, a depleted team, a converted atheist, a weird habit of checking license plates, and a business deal 2,566 miles from my office with a extremely-delayed closing to help soften someone's heart for sovereign ambush. And I wouldn't have had a chance to talk much to our guest had she not arrived after everyone else had.

It's happened since too—recently with a family from the next hill over from one where I had lived 34 years ago and 440 miles away. They pulled into the lot where I was serving, instead of any of the six lots covered by almost a dozen of my teammates. There aren't megachurches back in Athens, Pennsylvania; and I was able to make our church feel smaller to them.

To be fair, these moments aren't exclusive to when I'm in a reflective vest. I can't tell you how many times I've felt like I was in the right place at the right time for a divine encounter. I felt a tug to say something, to ask something, to walk over and introduce myself. I have new friends from those prompts. More importantly, there are people with a future in heaven now because of those moments.

Sadly, I need to confess the times I've passed on those assignments. With all the serendipity and wonder that's come from obedience to past prompting, you'd think I wouldn't balk. But I do. Just tonight, I wrestled with a tug to write a monster tip and "JESUS LOVES YOU" on the check in a pizza restaurant three time zones from home, where the server will never see me again. It was only a wrestle because I'm a coward. Tonight, I obeyed; but I'm guessing obedience to those assignments is more the exception than the rule in my life.

I've apologized to Jesus about watching called strikes instead of swinging on his pitches. I forget he wants to set me up for home runs. I forget that we both win when I swing, even when it seems I swing and miss.

What I'm trying to do now is to look at those moments like I look at those moments on a bungee platform, in an open airplane door, or in a kayak at the top of a set of whitewater rapids. When my legs feel heavy, when my heart beats almost loud enough to hear, when background noise blurs or roars—it's go time. What's about to happen is no accident.

Bring your helmet, Ryan. There just might be a collision.

NOT THE ARCTIC

Let's be known for our for-ness.

It's not easy to get to Antarctica. That was part of the continent's appeal for me.

The desire for remote destinations blossomed on my first international backpacking trip. My friend, Woody, led us up some grueling Argentina switchbacks to Laguna de los Tres, the glacier lake at the base of Fitz Roy. You've probably seen Fitz Roy and not known it. The iconic peak's silhouette comprises most of the logo for the adventure apparel brand, Patagonia. Because of the low-hanging cloud cover that had thankfully cooled our climb, we had the whole place to ourselves. In answer to some prayer, the clouds suddenly and completely parted, framing this incredible summit in blue; and the peak was reflected in the lake in front of us. We worshipped and took turns snapping some inadequate pictures. Woody warned me, "Those pictures won't mean as much to anyone else as they do to you. Unless you've stood here, you don't know what it took to get here."

He was right.

Since that time, I've sought out other places like Laguna de Los Tres—Norway's Runde Fyr, Middle Caicos's Mudjin Harbor, Vancouver Island's West Coast Trail, Italy's Via Ferrata Eterna, Kauai's Kalalau Trail, and the Santa Elena Canyon between Texas and Mexico. Standing in these remote places births a sense of pride and accomplishment; it also brings me to my knees. I feel connected with my own soul and closer to God. They confront my arrogance, challenge my priorities, and reveal the smallness of my dreams. I hope you've gotten to experience places and moments like that. If you have, you can imagine why Antarctica has called to me since high school.

The Drake Passage, where the Pacific and Atlantic Oceans collide, regularly offers rough sailing. Those who frequent the route affectionately call it "the Drake Shake." Our voyage to the frozen continent came with some extra adventure sauce. To get to the Antarctic Circle, our captains piloted the former Russian research vessel through a category 1 hurricane. Chugging along at five to eleven miles per hour, we climbed and slid down waves up to twenty-six feet tall. We lost a day of exploring because of those conditions on the way down.

To fill the time at sea, our expedition company offered live lectures from the various scientists and other content experts who would be guiding our pending excursions. I've forgotten almost everything I heard in those seminars on the *M/V Ortelius*, but one tidbit from Arjen Drost has reverberated in my heart and mind ever since.

The Dutch ornithologist towered over us, always leaning forward because of the low ceiling. The jolly, bald yeti of a professor asked those of us huddled around him if we knew how Antarctica got its name. Apparently, we all looked befuddled enough that he offered the answer.

"'Antarctica' simply means 'not the Arctic.'"

I was instantly embarrassed that this thought hadn't occurred to me instinctively. Right after that, I was struck by the notion that a massive, diverse, beautiful—breathtaking—place would be named for what it's not. A place where scientists constantly discover new realities is known for where it isn't.

I mostly tuned out the rest of the presentation, thinking instead about how this was indicative of the human experience. We live in a world where we categorize people by beliefs or behaviors and then define ourselves by how we're not like them. This is true of sports and pop culture, schools and professions, cultures and politics, philosophy and faith. I grew up in a religious sect that defined itself by what we didn't like, what we didn't read, what we didn't sing, what we didn't wear to church. While piously making claims about having a personal relationship with Jesus, we used a checklist to measure if our Eternal Groom was impressed enough to love us more than those we weren't like.

That's problematic. First, we can't impress God, especially with asceticism. Nothing we could ever give up could be compared with what Jesus gave up to rescue us. We can't even impress humans to love us. I've never done it, anyway—despite decades of trying. Also, measuring love is weird. There's no tape measure for that—no scale, no breathalyzer, no 3D scanner. Nobody keeps an Excel spreadsheet somewhere with love measurements over time. "Honey, this is really encouraging. In 2007, our love measured a 76.4. Last year, we charted out at 89.7. I think we should round up to 90. What do you think?" One thing your partner wouldn't think is anything amorous.

Rules and trust in relationships are inversely proportional. The more rules your relationship has, the less trust at least one of the parties owns. The more trust is involved, the fewer rules are needed. That's why the closer we get to Jesus, we're guided more by a desire to share his heart than by a checklist. We want to be for what Jesus is for.

After returning to shore and Internet access, a Google search revealed that Arjen was mostly right. Turns out, "Antarctica" more literally means "opposite the Arctic." Not just *not* the Arctic. Opposed 180°. There's a vibe that they aren't just different but maybe also contrary—juxtaposed *against* each other.

Who wants to oppose the Arctic? Who's against the top of the planet?

Probably the same kind of people that feel opposite of people with different skin colors, different sexual orientations, different interests and preferences, different socioeconomic realities, and different political philosophies. It's not just Westboro Baptist spewing claims about whom God is against. In my past, it's been me. And there are times when I wouldn't type or voice such declarations, but my behavior demonstrated that against-ness. The irony comes in the very short list of people Jesus actually stands against. His younger brother told us that Jesus resists the proud. His biographers all recorded that he rebuked pious, condescending, religious leaders. The first and last of the list of seven sins that the Hebrew king, Solomon, said God hates are pride and divisiveness.

Antarctica made me consider the irony of the term "polar opposites." I get that the Arctic and Antarctic are 180° from each other, but Earth's poles have a lot in common:

Lots of snow and ice? Check.

Bitter, inhospitable cold? Check.

Seasons with no day and no night? Check.

Fascinating native animals? Check.

Just the word *blubber*? Check.

Basically, one has polar bears; and one has penguins. One is comprised of several sovereign countries; one is an independent land mass protected by an international treaty. Other than some small details, though, they're more alike than they are different.

The same holds true for us humans, who are more alike than we are different. We have more in common with our "opposites" than we like to admit. Black skin isn't the opposite of white skin. Democrats aren't the opposite of Republicans. Atheists aren't the opposite of believers. Whether we are God's adopted children or not, we were all made in his image. Jesus isn't against any of these categories, because he loves everyone. His best friend in ministry, John, wrote about that fact a lot. And he loves us even though we're all less than him, often against him. Through a BCE prophet, Jesus said none of us have his thoughts. Through an AD prophet, Jesus said none of us have attained perfection. Jesus spent a lot of time with those different from him—because we're all different from him.

If we're opposite to anyone, it's Jesus. And Jesus is *for* us. He's for *all* of us. He wants more for all of us. Ever since he lost the innocence and intimacy of his friendship with Adam and Eve, he's been going out of his way to woo us back to close friendship. He's for the things that will make that happen: acceptance and contrition, empathy and forgiveness, compassion and encouragement, humility and wholesomeness, hope and courage. He appeared to a rabbi named Saul, someone whose life mission was actually against Jesus; and he confronted Saul's against-ness. That Saul later wrote that Jesus' *kindness* is what leads us to repentance. Our surrender is a response to what Jesus is *for*. Our submission is an embrace of his robust for-ness. On our journey, he changes rts towards the people he loves, toward the reclamation he's *for*.

sus demonstrated this for-ness by attending the parties of the secular and the self-medicators. He asked the ashamed for a favor. He touched the weak and the contagious. He doodled in the dirt next to the accused. He let a mourning woman wipe her hair on his skin. He chose to die with criminals. He asked God to forgive both his torturers and their audience laden with *Schadenfreude*. He invited the hand of a doubter to touch his wounds. Then he left the planet and asked us to do the same in his name.

It's not enough to be known as a for-er instead of an against-er, though that's a good start. Jesus calls us to be for what he is for. I really wrestle with this. He's for different things than I am, better things than I'm for. He regularly reminds me of that for-ness. One of the most indelible of those reminders came on my fortieth birthday.

I had worked it all out—fourteen months in advance of the big day. On the morning of my birthday, I would park cars at church with my buddies and then run to catch my first flight toward Antarctica. Almost to the hour, I would start my forties on my way to the bottom of the world. I'm for adventure, for epic vacations, and for those social media thumbs and hearts. Jesus, though, is for Advent.

Almost a year before we were to set sail, our captain pushed our voyage back ten days. Between you and me, I was bummed. There went my birthday plans.

Eight months after the captain's postponement, a guy named Chris totaled his car while intoxicated. With blood and glass on his face, he told God he was done running his own life and would start saying yes to what Heaven asked. He walked into our church and heard a sermon about serving. He inquired at our welcome center and got connected with our parking lot team. In our pre-serving prayer huddle, he heard mention of a prayer and Bible study group and asked for an invite. Several weeks later on the asphalt a few feet from where he asked for that invite, Chris asked a new Father for forgiveness and invited Jesus to be the king of his life.

While people in our church are welcomed to get baptized in rivers, ponds, lakes, and pools with smaller gatherings, we host four baptism celebration weekends a year in our full adult and student assemblies. In the autumn climate where we live, one of those indoor parties is the better option in November; and Chris's "big room" baptism got scheduled for the Sunday after my birthday. A stranger just months before, he asked me to baptize him. I got the incredible privilege of speaking a benediction over him and pulling him up out of that water—because I wasn't in Antarctica.

Jesus knew I wasn't dreaming *for* enough.

He orchestrated something beautiful and eternal in spite of myself. He added advent to my adventure.

He does that a lot—and not just when I'm on vacation. My buddies tell me stories almost every week of Jesus injecting sovereign moments into their work, their gym time, their reunions with old friends, the stands at their kid's sporting events, and their conversations with vendors at the house. I hope you experience those advent moments too. The challenge for me and my friends is to set aside the things we were for right before those moments: our work deadlines, our lunch breaks, our scheduled extracurricular activities. Sometimes, it gets even harder. Every so often, God asks us to give up aspirations and former priorities, comfort and closed friend groups. I can tell you first hand, though, that people who have felt us being for them have often discovered that Jesus is for them.

While Antarctica is hauntingly beautiful and ruggedly indelible, nothing I did or saw down there compares to the feeling of seeing someone surrender to the One who is most for them. Swapping our fors with God's fors is worth it. It's not just an upgrade. It's where fulfillment and legacy overlap on a Venn diagram. It's joy. It's serendipity. It's electricity. It's a jaw-dropping place that pictures can't capture, and only the people who've stood there can understand. Thankfully, it's also a place we all are invited to visit, even though we might have to sail through a hurricane on our way there.

THE REAL DEAL

"Where you buy dis?"

A few weeks after I returned from Antarctica, I got antsy. You know what it's like when you have a gift card or tax refund burning a hole in your pocket? Or when you have one payment left on a loan—something you just can't wait to cross off the list? That was me but turned up to eleven. I came home from visiting my sixth continent and having made friends with people who had just collected all seven.

I needed Asia to complete the set. So, I started Googling places to paraglide on the planet's largest continent. For my clients' sake, I normally plan vacations half a year or more in advance; but I couldn't sit still. It was my annual slow season, and my credit card points might as well have been blinking on my screen. I settled on Pokhara, Nepal, where my friends Dolma and Tashi lived.

Most people visit Pokhara on their way to treks in the Annapurna region of the Himalaya Mountains. Or, like me, they come to paraglide with Machapuchare ("Fishtail") Mountain in the backdrop.

I've never seen sunrises like I saw on the roof of my hotel. With Australian music playing in my headphones, I watched a blurry orange sun push through the haze of a burgeoning metropolis, where almost every city block had a building in some state of construction or renovation. The sunsets begged for attention too, turning everything magenta and then purple over Fewa Lake.

Because of the low loud cover, I ended up paragliding only once in Pokhara. I spent most of my time writing blog posts, napping, and exploring local cultural sites. Halfway through my week in Nepal, I had purchased three down jackets and a 40-liter backpack—all with a The North Face logo embroidered on them and all from tiny stores that spill out onto dusty sidewalks through open garage doors. For those four items, I had spent a total of $82; and I had knowingly overpaid, because I hate negotiating.

I don't know how the official The North Face store on this same lakeside market in Pokhara stays in business. Just their graphic tees started at $30 a pop.

An embroidered The North Face logo appeared everywhere I looked in Pokhara. The label was worn by almost everyone. My taxi driver told me he made the equivalent of $140 a month, and he was probably wearing The North Face. My taxi livery guy did. The waiters at the brick oven pizza place I frequented wore red fleece sweatshirts as a uniform, and the logo on their chest was not that of the restaurant but of The North Face.

The inventories of those trekker shops included a light smattering of Mammut and Arc'teryx and a brand I didn't recognize but assumed came from Europe. No Columbia or Marmot, though. No Patagonia, either.

In the shop where I purchased the backpack, the tiny, gruff shopkeeper pointed at my heart and asked "Where you buy dis?" On the other end of her pointed finger was the Patagonia logo on my puffy. A patch three-fourths the size of my pinky finger told her I was different from her other customers.

She could have been asking to see if a local competitor had just grabbed a competitive advantage or to size up how rich of an American I was. Or both. I took her question in a different way. In a retail corridor overflowing with what I assumed were all knockoffs, she could've been asking if I had the real deal.

Isn't that the question our culture is asking?

We all carry a sneaking suspicion that people around us live behind façades on social media. We're so entrenched in constant entertainment that we just assume everything else on our screens is artificial or at least superficial. When political and media personalities want to dismiss people who agree with them, they don't yell, "That's wrong!" No, they claim the assertions are "*fake* news." We all concede that "reality show" is an ironic if not an oxymoronic label for unscripted television shows. If you pay attention to the end credits on all of those unscripted shows, you'll find every one of those shows has *writers*—not to give participants lines to say but to craft a narrative that wouldn't be there if we watched the raw footage.

Let that sink in a second.

We now have gender-specific apps for upgrading our Instagram photos. A celebrity on the cover of two adjacent magazines in the Target checkout lane can look very different because each has its own photo editor. We don't know if rock stars are actually singing on Saturday Night Live or how accurate their studio albums are. So many online daters have been duped by fake love interests that society had to give the practice a name: catfishing. Now, every celebrity's child has to ask their parents if they got into their college on merit or because of expensive, improper strings that have been pulled. Scores of Olympic or professional athletes are busted each year—not just for performance-enhancing drugs but also for the drugs known to mask them. A growing number of religious celebrities are telling us our holy books aren't completely valid. Famous pastors are constantly found to have lived double lives that included grievous addictions, shadowy financial practices, and predatory abuse. Many more clergy members have not been caught yet because they don't have a big enough spotlight to illuminate the cracks.

We are surrounded by filters and fakeness and post-production. Influencers have made cliché the camera angles that make butts look rounder, thigh gaps look wider, and double chins pull taut. Our vacation pictures never look like those professional ones online. "That's a composite image," my wife, a professional photographer, warned when I showed her a cool backpacking photo on Instagram.

My niece side hustles as a makeup artist. Earlier in the day on which I'm writing this chapter, I asked Cheyenne if she shows before and after photos of her clients in her marketing. She told me she posts only the after photos because she doesn't want her customers to feel duplicitous—even though their friends all know they look like Kylie Jenner only on special occasions.

We all know the game. We quickly recognize others who are playing the same game. That's why authenticity has become a currency. When people take their masks off—or discard their masks altogether—everyone takes notice. "Where you buy dis?" they ask.

You can't buy authenticity, though. You can't manufacture it, either.

You definitely can't fake it. People have tried that and flamed out. Or they've not tried it—curating a persona—and found it mostly empty.

I have.

Careful public editing can build your personal brand. It can even open doors to careers and adventures, but it very easily becomes a covetous competition, a hungry addiction, and a thief of joy. I don't have enough distance from myself yet to know if I'm in recovery or just on the verge of it. I see the pitfalls all around me because I've fallen in them more times than I can count. I'm thankful that the awareness has moved to sensitivity and maybe even to healing. This issue became so huge for me that I engaged the help of a professional counselor to help me untangle the knots. One of the themes from my weekly conversations with Lindsey has been how much effort I put into chasing acceptance and how I've thoroughly blurred the line between authenticity and persona. Then there's the whole question of whether I'm using Jesus for my brand or my brand for him. Between you and me, that enigma has been the biggest threat to this book being published.

The challenge in pursuing authenticity is that it requires me to bow out, to leave the game. That game is so rewarding when you have winning hands, and I somehow get those cards a lot. Jesus told a rich, 30-under-30-list guy to sell everything in order to determine who and what held his heart. I'm not sure if that austerity was descriptive or prescriptive for the rest of us, but I know Jesus still asks all of us to check our idols at the door.

For me, that's the game. For you, that might be something completely different. For all of us, though, it will require that we love Jesus more than we love accomplishment—no matter the accomplishment you chase. What I've found is that the more I fall in love with him, I grow closer to the person he destined me to be, for you to be, for us to be. Our true selves. That becomes attractive to people in love with lesser gods.

I hope people ask me some version of "Where you buy dis?" for the rest of my life. I want to be starkly known as a genuine person, the real Ryan George. As I obey what Jesus and the early church fathers have admonished, I'm finding legacy beyond Facebook feedback. As I unveil my struggles with true friends and let them share theirs with me, I'm finding fulfillment and intimacy like never before. As I reveal my journey online, I find more meaning in my life offline. Life feels more real, if that makes sense.

That shouldn't be surprising. Jesus called himself the Way, the Truth, and the Life. When we live in the way of love where truth is the default setting, it makes sense that life follows. With everyone searching for what's real, finding it offers an exhale of relaxation. Candor for the sake of candor can be annoying and even hurtful, but confident vulnerability works like a lighthouse above dark waves. Jesus designed our current reality so that our souls would find rescue and rest in that light rather than in the shadows. It's tempting to market our faith life as a buttoned-up and manicured prosperity, but Jesus didn't ask us to sell that message. He didn't ask us to promote anything. He didn't leave any advertising strategies or hashtag recommendations. He didn't design any labels for our jackets.

Jesus called us to speak the truth in love, knowing that concoction would lead to a countercultural life of authenticity and compassion. My guess is that he foresaw how generations of weary souls would be drawn to him through disciples ready to answer some version of the question, "Where you buy dis?"

FINDING PEACE IN A TRASH CAN

Wear your harness, but don't hold onto it.

Several years ago, I fell off a mountain with a trash can over my head.

I was told later that I plummeted 197 feet before the line that connected me to something solid pulled taut, and I swung out over a remote New Zealand canyon. I didn't have to be told later that the darkness inside the container multiplied my fear. My muscles clenched, frozen in desperation. My yelling came from further down in my chest than my voice usually does—maybe because my stomach had clogged my throat. That inarticulate noise reverberated all around my head, reminding me I was trapped.

At the Shotover Canyon Swing, you can pay to fall off a mountain more than a dozen different ways, including strapped to a plastic lawn chair. For my second "jump," I chose the affectionately named "Bin Laden" option. The jumpmasters placed a trash bin over my shoulders and clipped it to my harness, pinning my arms straight down at my side. I could hear a series of metallic punctuation, the clipping and unclipping of carabiners in the transition from the safety line to the wire that would swing me 600 feet out across a river 350 feet below the cliff where I stood.

Through the Rubbermaid straitjacket, I heard, "Start walking. You'll know when you're off the mountain." They continued to click things—decoy sounds I would later learn. As I dropped into an utter frenzy, one of the jumpmasters exclaimed, "Wait! We had one more!"

The helplessness that overtook me felt like the first few seconds of a car accident. I shouted, hoping for catharsis. I waited for an impact. The darkness doubled the wait, slowing reality like it was being narrated for someone else. The unknown outcome loomed as scary as the reality I had witnessed earlier: exposed rocks hundreds of feet down.

When gravity brought me to the end of the slack in my safety line, I flew out between the canyon walls. In that moment, the ride harkened back to playground sensations—back and forth, out and back—just with longer passes between the forward and backward motion. A minute later, a winch cranked me back up to solid ground. I joked with my jumpmasters about their verbal prank, knowing I got more adrenaline because they had added more fear than I had brought with me.

I had stepped out on faith that they had taken care of everything from their relatively sovereign view of the canyon. That trust didn't take away my fear. It didn't mitigate my falling or remove the darkness. Without that faith, though, I would never have experienced that incredible moment. I would've missed out on the euphoria and wonder and accomplishment that pulsed through those recently frozen muscles. I would've bypassed a story that enriched my life.

Ceding control led me to a new and better reality.

That truth didn't hit me at the moment. That realization hit years later while I was sitting in a barber chair. The rotation of stylists who regularly cut my hair all keep notes on their computer system of how I like my fade and the weird way I prefer my beard trimmed. They might also save conversation notes in there too, because they always ask me about my next trip or most recent adventure. After answering their question, I redirect the conversation, asking them about what adventures they have on the horizon or their life to-do list.

Mary Ann told me she wants to try skydiving. First, I affirmed that goal and told her the safest place to do it here in Virginia—the company with an instructor who has held the record for most jumps by an American female. She runs the tandem skydiving school that didn't break my buddy's back and didn't kill a woman in my church. Then, I told Mary Ann she should jump tandem the first time. "There's too much to remember when you jump by yourself," I explained. "Tandem jumps let you soak in everything around you, because someone else is worrying about all the details."

That advice rings ironic from my voice. I'm addicted to control. In most areas of my life, I trust myself way more than I trust others—even people I care about.

I'm writing this chapter next to a series of small waterfalls on an autumn evening. I wish I had brought my backpack. I carried my blanket, laptop, laptop charger, extra hoodie, and water bottle out here in my arms. Stepping from rock to rock between the pour-overs, I thought to myself, *I probably wouldn't trust someone else to carry all of this stuff out here. I would feel anxious the whole time if they did.* That's where the irony comes into play. See, I'm a klutz. I've ruined two laptops because of my lack of dexterity and situational awareness. If Jesus weren't sovereign and omnipotent, he'd probably chew his fingernails watching me maneuver out here.

My charade of self-reliance is laughable, especially in light of my track record. I've made tens of thousands of dollars' worth of mistakes as the only employee I've trusted with my business. I've wrecked and totaled cars when I insisted on driving. People hire me every week to advertise real estate for them, and I told my wife she should trust my real estate intuition. Then, I promptly lost my retirement savings, an inheritance, and my business' cash reserves on our last house. I designed our current house and took great pride in that feat until it literally sank and pulled apart at various seams. Interpersonally, I've made matters worse while attempting to deliver remedy. I can't get out of my own way more days than not.

Too often, I want God's help without his intervention. I'd love for him to be an instructor—just not my tandem pilot. I don't mind being harnessed to him, but I usually want my hands in the steering toggles. I'm more open to advice from his experience than in surrendering the control held by my ignorance.

Thankfully, Jesus is patient with me. Long-suffering, actually. He keeps giving me object lessons about this control issue. The stack of them is deeper than the twenty-year collection of *National Geographic* magazines my mom once bought at a yard sale.

With both my canyon swing jumpmasters and my skydiving tandem instructors, my gratitude soared after I placed my full trust in their hands. The constraints of those harnesses actually led to freedom. Letting someone else take care of the details helped me better absorb the scenery and the physical sensations. When I behaved as though what I hadn't yet experienced was true, new truth revealed itself to me in high-definition color and stereo surround sound. When I embraced the mystery, obedience grew scarier but also simpler.

Just let go.

If you're like me, you have the theology part down. You grasp that Jesus doesn't need faith because he can see what we can't. You too, probably assume he can see the future. If there is a grand plan, he definitely has the PDF readily available. Probably right on his desktop. His method isn't obscured by any madness. My dysfunction doesn't mess up what Sovereignty is doing. (Neither does yours.)

When my faith breaks down, it's the practical application where it all falls apart.

I've experienced The Instructor's sovereignty in everyday life, when I've obeyed what he said. I've been most grateful for that sovereignty when I've adhered to counterintuitive instructions when his voice whispered weird orders. That stuff made sense only after I put it into practice.

I remember one Monday morning when a small obedience led to an indelible encounter with Sovereignty. I was swimming laps at the YMCA when I felt inundated by an unshakeable prompt to pray for my friend, Mountz—right there, right then, while I was still in the pool. I hadn't seen Mountz in a while and didn't know of any pressing needs in his life, but I felt compelled to pray for something specific. When I got out of the locker room, I texted him about my weird assignment and the specific request I had felt led to pray for him. Mountz immediately texted back, "Call me right now." I did, and he told me the reason for that timing and the story I didn't know but had prayed over. We both left that conversation with goosebumps, impressed by a personal and active God. I don't remember now what I prayed. I don't remember anymore what Mountz's need was at that moment. I just remember that immediate obedience made me feel connected to Jesus on a heart level—emotionally, not just religiously.

Despite all of the times like that morning when I've gotten it right, obedience still isn't my default setting. Even though God's goodness has become best-ness over and over again, I still try to carry my mess on the rocks of my life instead of giving it the One Who Created the Rocks. Because his promises are true, though, he keeps rewarding those exceptions. My guess is that he's hoping that the resulting peace becomes first sweet and then addictive to me. I'm definitely seeing the pattern more often than ever and closer to real time than in my past.

The Apostle Paul wrote that God's peace surpasses our understanding, but that doesn't mean we can't experience it. We can feel it right after we relinquish our control to a good Father, to the One with immutable sovereignty. When gravity pulls on our trash can, when our help is behind us, and when wind buffets our shaky feet, we can still enjoy a reward we can't fully explain. When the mystery is dark, when we hear reverberations of our own voice instead of his, and when our feet dangle far from solid ground, Jesus will meet us in our difficult obedience with immeasurable sensations.

When we do what Jesus asks, he does what he promised.

When we embrace the mystery, Jesus reveals himself.

When we put our hands up, he gives us something too big for them to hold.

JACK'S PACK

Carry your corner of the mat.

Along a forty-seven-mile stretch of coastline on Vancouver Island, more than a hundred ships have met their demise. So many survivors walked back to civilization on the inhospitable edge of its rocky, uninhabited shores that a rescue trail formed just inside the temperate rainforest. At some point, Parks Canada and probably a bevy of volunteers built an incredible system of bridges, boardwalks, ladders, and cable car crossings between the trailheads. It's now simply called the West Coast Trail.

Rated as the top North American hike without a mountain, it's not for the faint of heart. Just imagine doing a Tough Mudder or Spartan Race with a week's worth of food and camping gear on your back. Now do that six days in a row without a shower or flushing toilet.

The public trail is so treacherous that when we hiked it, only fifty-two people per day were permitted to start hiking on it; and all of those hikers were required to pay $150 for emergency services. The trail is open only five or six months a year, yet an average of almost eighty backpackers get medically evacuated each season.

I brought a client and seven guys from my church to this bucket-list hike. Our group included a former member of Special Forces, a former wilderness guide trained by Outward Bound, and at least one Eagle Scout. Three of the guys had engineering day jobs; two worked on a church staff. We represented multiple points on the spiritual spectrum. Other hikers we encountered labeled us, "The Virginia Nine."

The trail lived up to the hype. I remember just one of the sets of ladders held 220 rungs. That's not a typo. 220. We trudged through sand and jumped from stumps and logs across mud bogs. Almost all of us slipped and fell and had bruises to prove it. At one point, when the tide surprised us, we had to traverse a large rock outcropping while hanging above the lapping waves. No ropes. No safety cables. Just lateral bouldering with full trekking packs on.

My sleeping bag fell out there and dropped into the ocean. I slept that night in all of my Under Armour layers and rain gear, shivering and using my backpack as a sleeping bag for my legs. The following night I had a new sleeping bag, but it came at a significant cost.

We awoke that morning and conferred with the guidebook. It told us to pack extra potable water because there wouldn't be any clean water sources until we got to our campsite at the end of the day. For most of the West Coast Trail, you can hike either the waterfront or the official trail just inside the rainforest. We filled all of our water bottles and headed out toward the shoreline. With the tide out, we navigated along a rock shelf. The surface texture of that shelf included both slick stone and sharp edges. This shelf's rocks had been both smoothed by the sea and eroded into coarse crags.

Beautiful anemone, black mussels, and a rainbow of starfish hid in some of the pools and under the shadow of some of the rocks. The ocean crashed to our left as the sun popped up over the trees on our right. We had subdivided into several conversation groups. As we walked and talked, individuals and groups alike stopped to absorb one aspect of our surroundings or just take in a sweeping view of the surreal landscape. There was no path, no cairns, no explicitly correct way to traverse the shelf. So, we all followed our curiosity in the same general direction but significantly spaced apart.

Until Jack fell.

Jack and Aaron's conversation abruptly changed when Jack's foot slipped. As he fell forward, the extra water now in the top of his pack drove his head into the rock at his feet. The impact gave him a concussion and a gash in his forehead. He didn't yell or cry, but we were all soon assembled next to him as his blood dripped onto the rock. We combined our emergency medical kits, and the former EMT in our group started patching him up.

Our tech guru, John, somehow got cell signal from the Olympic Peninsula across the Strait of Juan de Fuca, called emergency services, and gave them our location. They told him they could send a helicopter. If we could get him to a specific beach, though, they could extract him by Zodiac boat. "Jack, can you make it three miles?" one of us asked.

He said he could. So, John scheduled the rendezvous. The park rangers gave us two and a half hours to get there. Jack stood up, donned his pack, and gave it a go for about a mile. Eventually, dizziness overtook him. Seeing him woozy and a little light-headed, the rest of us decided to share the responsibility of his pack until we got to the more level terrain on the way to the extraction point. That was no small feat, considering some of the terrain we faced would be stout with just our own packs. At times, we built a bucket brigade to get his pack and ours up, down, and over treacherous sections. At least one section required a rope. I remember my turn, carrying his pack on my front with my pack on my back, using trekking poles to steady myself.

On our backpacking trips, each guy takes a day leading a spiritual encounter. Since Jack would be leaving us, he volunteered to give his homily on the bluff above the rendezvous beach. As the red rescue boat appeared on the horizon, Jack had his back to the water in the midst of sharing Scripture and his heart. I couldn't concentrate on his words, distracted by his pending departure. He got to a stopping point, and we interjected, "Your boat is here." I can't remember if we rushed a prayer or just rushed to the beach.

The rescue team inspected and approved Woody's bandage work and gave Jack a Mustang rescue suit for the full throttle Zodiac trip to the dock for the ambulance transfer. We snapped a group picture with our favorite Army Ranger and then took turns hugging him in the way guys do: finishing with big slaps on the back.

Jack let me borrow his sleeping bag for the rest of the trip. He checked into our hostel a few days early and spent the time reading his Bible and talking to God about his disappointment of not finishing with us. He told us later that he found this sequestered time to be refreshing and soul-filling—that the jaw-dropping nature on the trail had actually gotten in between him and his Creator. But he let us know he would return someday to hike the trail in reverse to make sure he conquered the whole thing. I might just join him now that I know how to pack lighter and have experience with the tide charts.

What I learned the most from Jack's accident, though, was a picture of what it means to "bear one another's burden." Jesus asked us all to do that because spiritual adventures often require it. I'm not sure if it's built into the process, but it sure happens a lot. Most, if not all, of us take turns tripping, hurting ourselves, and adding a slow section to our spiritual journey. Sometimes it's a mistake or a result of ignorance. At other times it's a willful detour. Many times it's not even our fault. People or health or other circumstances we can't control create a situation too heavy for us to bear alone.

If you've ever needed a burden carried, you know that can mean a million different things. It might be someone else being a cocon-spirator, a prayer partner, a safe place to share a secret. Maybe it's sitting in a hospital room or courtroom with you—or on the side of the road. It could look like a MealTrain, a series of encouragement cards, or just a day away from your difficult reality. I've seen it look like a surprise home remodel, an army carrying moving boxes, and donated car repairs. For me at times, it's just been someone listening.

Jesus gave us scores of calls to do things as one another, with one another, for one another. Those commands are all ways of lightening each other's burdens. Somewhere, I heard that most of those *you* commands in the New Testament should actually be translated to *y'all*—as in, "Y'all do this together." In our bootstrap, individualistic culture, sometimes doing a thing together with others is as hard as just doing the thing at all. I wouldn't be surprised if that's the point.

Jesus often speaks to us through the voices in our lives. Sometimes he reveals himself and his way in others' burdens and in the burden of otherness. He knows sharing a burden will slow us down, but that's at least part of the objective. Even when we're heading in the right direction, we can miss important moments when we're in a hurry. I'm not sure I've ever read about Jesus being in a hurry. He's been to the future and back and is content to walk slowly with us. He does this for both the direct experience but also as an example because walking slowly with him often means walking slowly with others.

The Bible's writers didn't call us to codependence. It doesn't say we have to carry someone's burden all by ourselves or all the time. The guys who carried the lame man to Jesus showed us that we just need to carry one corner of someone's mat until they're back on their feet. And maybe we take turns—even on our one corner of the mat.

As in that lame man's encounter with Jesus and our situation with Jack, you'll find the objective is often just to get someone to professional help. I've had to tell several of my buddies, "That's above my pay grade, man." Thankfully, God's not opposed to incorporating doctors, counselors, attorneys, and contractors in his intervention. He can get glory from leveraging the talents and experiences he gave those pros. That doesn't mean we get absolved from accepting, supporting, and comforting; but we can get people with specific strengths to help us carry the burden.

Even the Special Forces people in our lives will need our help. Even as Army Rangers, we'll eventually need someone to carry our pack. It can be hard to allow others to love us that way. Well—not to speak for you—it's challenging for me. Being on the team that helped Jack, though, showed me that those moments are pregnant with potential moments of Advent. Those times of connection through sharing a need are teeming with adventure. That friction, that sweat, and that carefulness make the path more memorable. We notice more details in the process. We feel part of a grand, sovereign plan. The teamwork gives the story more dynamic characters and a more interesting plot.

Imagine that: Jesus giving us a better story than we would've written ourselves.

AN ADVENTURE I CAN'T PROVE

You're going to need two hands for this.

A few Augusts ago, I crossed an item off my bucket list. With my 71-year-old pastor and my close friend, Aaron, I climbed the *Via Ferrata Eterna* in the Dolomites, Italy's jaw-dropping section of the Alps. The Italians invented *via ferrata* and started the concept with routes that are still impressive. They developed the mountain-scaling system of rungs and safety cables for troop movement over rugged mountain terrain in World War I, and their "iron way" is still some of the best in the world.

The afternoon before we started on the trail that would eventually lead us to the *Via Ferrata Eterna*, Aaron and I decided to get an aerial preview of what was to come. In paragliders. We rode with our tandem pilots in a gondola up near the top of Plose, a ski resort on a nearby mountain.

If you've never been paragliding, you have to know that its practitioners are typically chill men and women. I've flown tandem with at least seven different pilots, and six of them portrayed a resting heart rate of forty beats per minute. They had their heads on a swivel but never in panic or concern. While their altimeters beeped, it never seemed to surprise them.

The exception to that was Joe, my pilot at Plose. First, I tripped during takeoff; and the canopy dragged me along the grass until I got my feet back under me. Then, Joe seemed super concerned that we didn't catch the thermal updraft that Aaron and his pilot caught to extend the flight and give better views. Joe apologized after repeatedly looking over his shoulder at our friends. Then in his broken English, he told me we had two remaining options for the tour. We could gently circle Brixen, the nearest city, at roughly our current altitude. Or we could do a "proximity flight" down the face of the mountain. He explained the second option with a zig-zagging hand pointed at the ski slopes behind us. I'd seen proximity flights online from similar Alp locations, but I'd never been offered one next to a mountain.

My heart leaped. A grin expanded across my face.

I indicated my preference for the latter, even though that would result in a shorter flight. (In any adventure you try in the sky, the more aerobatics you do, the faster you lose altitude.) Joe approved of my choice. He collapsed his selfie stick, clipped it and its camera to our harness, and then warned that both of us would have to hold on with both hands.

This is about to get good.

Joe pulled a hard right, and we dove down just over the trees. Then, we flew over a slope-side hotel—close enough that I would've been able to tell who was on their back deck if I knew any of the people there. Then, we pulled a hard left. We spun 180 degrees and dove further down over the resort and buzzed the people in the pool. Joe was smiling now, and so was I.

He pulled the right toggle, and we twisted over to one of the ski slopes. Below the treetops, we raced down what I'd guess would be blue ski runs during the winter. Grass as tall as a toddler reached for our shoes as our hands likewise rose above our heads. We slid straight down the slopes like we were bombing 'em in a bobsled. Every once in a while, Joe yanked one side of the wing down to fly through a gap or around a corner. Our feet rose as our shoulders dipped through the curve. I'd flown this close to the ground in a fan-powered paraglider but never in one propelled by gravity.

Eventually, we got to the air above Joe's farm. He transitioned us back to a gentle glide, gracefully circling over his lush fields. Then we glided to the drop zone in a park on the edge of the city. We slid onto the grass with wide grins on our faces. It was one of the best paragliding flights of my life, and I have no pictures or videos of the best part.

I can't tell you how many times—like that Saturday evening—that I've missed the adventure scripted on my itinerary but found Sovereignty had better plans.

On a regular basis, Jesus swaps out an adrenaline rush with a moment of transcendence. Throughout my spiritual journey, Omniscience has replaced an accomplishment with a sense of purpose. In moments of clarity, Jesus has changed out a pursuit for contentment. No matter how many times he does this, I still desperately chase control. Too often, I still don't let go of things I can't imagine he can improve.

Maybe that's why one of the things that often bring my body or soul to its knees is pondering God's patience. Out on hikes, one of my most common prayers is "Thank you for waiting on me, for not giving up." One of the reasons I journal and blog and even write this book is to capture the stories he's writing from either his intervention or my surrender. Or both. I need to retrace the steps when his sovereignty arrived in my life as seeming serendipity, how he grabbed the wheel to take me on a more scenic road. My lack of faith needs to reread tales of the goodness of his heart, the trustworthiness of his ways.

Like Joe, though, Jesus still lets us choose the route to our next landing spot. That blows my mind. He knows better but doesn't force the issue. Whether we've soared above the mountains like our fortunate friends or missed our opportunities, he lets us decide between the commonplace and the spectacular for the rest of our flight. He gives us the choice between a comfortable, photogenic distance and an action-packed proximity. "Hold on," he whispers. "This is about to get good."

Think about the times in our lives when we're advised to use both hands.

- cradling our newborn sibling
- carrying a bowl to the dining room table
- holding onto the chains of a swing
- gripping a tee ball bat
- holding a candle at a vigil
- pushing a lawn mower or swinging the trimmer
- guiding a steering wheel
- eating that monster burger in a famous tourist spot
- pushing a friend's car out of the snow
- sliding fabric through a sewing machine
- holding onto a tow rope behind a boat
- wrapping our arms around the driver on an ATV or motorcycle or snowmobile
- connecting to our bride or groom at our wedding

Those are beautiful or at least colorful moments. They are over-flowing with important, indelible memories. Someone else might have stood in the background snapping pictures, but our recollections pull from internal footage, the action captured inches from our face. With both of our hands in front of us, we focused on the adventure within our grasp. We pursued the moment just to have it, to live it, to know how it feels.

Jesus came to give us more of those abundant moments. He claimed to be the Way, the Truth, and the Life. It shouldn't surprise us, then, when he steers us to the truest moments brimming over with vivid humanity. He continually invites us to let go of one-handed endeavors for more two-handed ones.

My entire adult life, I've heard people preach and pray about being the "hands and feet of Jesus." That's always been a scary idea for me. Jesus touched lepers and walked to a cross. In contrast, I root for Jesus to hike around my favorite disc golf course a bunch. I really want his left foot jumping back and forth between the clutch and the brake on a winding mountain road. I want him to hold the things I crave. I hope he group hugs people I like into a touch football huddle. I want aerobatics *and* proof for social media, but I'd like to keep my distance from pain and poverty, rubble and tragedy, brokenness and discomfort. I want two mutually exclusive realities.

One of the great tensions of life is that pull in both directions. Unless it's just me, it seems like we all want both impact and safety. But meaning and popularity are usually at the end of different train tracks. Influence and comfort are often destinations of different planes, even if from adjacent departure gates. We can't hold control and surrender at the same time. Gripping materialism in one hand and transcendence in the other will lead to a painful stretch until something slips or tears or snaps.

Maybe that's why Jesus invites us to place both of our hands into the toggles connected to his canopy. His banner over us is love. He wants what's best for our lives and the ensuing lives we'll touch. He knows the closer we are to the needs around us, the more likely we are to engage with them. He trusts that the closer we fly to situations that break his heart, the more of our heart he has a chance to occupy. He knows if we drop the camera and hold on with both hands, he can steer us to places we wouldn't have experienced on our own. We won't be able to show others what it was like. We'll probably inadequately describe them. But we'll tell those stories again and again—because that's where we felt alive.

COLD RAMEN IN THE CLOUDS

The Gospel everyone craves.

In 2012, a *Backpacker* cover story featured the top 10 American camp-sites reachable in a single day from a major American city. I kept that issue on my desk for more than a year, regularly staring at the cover photo. In it, an orange tent perched on the edge of what looked like a tall cliff; and rows of jagged mountain peaks filled the background.

The magazine's editors weren't overselling it. As I dreamed for three years about setting my tent there, I filled a Pinterest board with other photographers' shots from that same vantage point. I turned my computer's wallpaper to a picture of the wildflower-lined path up Sahale Mountain, on which the tent sites were perched. I followed Sahale visitors on Instagram. I've lived a bucket list kind of life, but camping there rested near the top of my to-do list for three years.

Until Wednesday, August 8, 2015, when I crossed it off the list.

Two days prior, I flew out to Seattle and drove into the North Cascades in hopes of nabbing one of a handful of backcountry tent sites below the Sahale Glacier. At the time, the spots were not reservable more than a day in advance; and all reservations had to be secured in person. On less than three hours of sleep, I raced from the airport to the ranger station. There, I learned from a kind ranger that they had no permits available that day. "We have one left for tomorrow night, though. Do you want that?" she asked.

"Yes, ma'am. I'll take it. I flew all the way out here for this site." What I didn't tell the ranger is that I had also bought a DSLR camera, an ultralight tripod, multiple GoPro accessories, a powerful headlamp, crampons, glacier glasses, new hiking shoes, a new (more photogenic) tent, and other gear for the express purpose of documenting this expedition and looking good in that documentation.

She gave me some suggestions for hikes and campsites to fill the day at hand, assigned my portable bear canister, and handed me the coveted backcountry permit to attach to my pack.

I awoke the next morning with the realization that my stove was not functional. In my rush from the airport, I had purchased the wrong kind of fuel canister. More than an hour past a store that probably had one and needing to start my ascent early, I gave up on hot meals and— more importantly—celebratory hot cocoa at base camp. I packed the stove in my rental car, went through my gear with a mental checklist, and then started on the switchbacks up to the tree line.

The forecast for the campsite's altitude—in August—showed a high of 39°F and clouds until the following morning. Undeterred, I carried all my camera gear with the hope of a Thursday morning photo shoot.

Halfway to the top, the clouds started lifting. I wondered if they might burn off, as they had on other backpacking trips. The trail climbed steeper. As I reached an exposed section, gusts of wind enveloped me. I could see a large bank of clouds approaching—first two ridgelines away, then just one ridgeline away, and then between me and the next row of mountains. I could also see two groups of backpackers behind and below me. I pushed myself to keep my lead on them. I had encountered multiple groups descending from Sahale Glacier Camp, and my math indicated I might get my pick of the campsites. I might get *the* site, the one featured in the magazine.

The clouds arrived as I got to the boulder field, and they brought a driving mist. As I neared the scree slope for the final ascent, cold rain soaked my upwind pant leg and pelted my rain jacket. The slapping rain stopped long enough only for snowflakes to scurry around me. A minute or two later, the precipitation transitioned back to rain. My hands stung from the cold, but I had to keep them out of my pockets for balance on the steep, slippery gravel.

There was little relief when I found the campsite, because I had to erect a tent in sustained winds of no less than twenty miles per hour. My trembling hands were so cold that it hurt to don my gloves (which were soaked in less than a minute, anyway). I took a visual sweep of the area: no other tents, though visibility was limited. Then I jumped into my tent. Other than a quick bladder break, I didn't leave that tent for more than sixteen hours.

Inside my tent, I shivered until my 0°F sleeping bag and foil emergency blanket got to full heat. I snacked on some cold, dry ramen noodles, fooled around on my phone, and then fell asleep.

I woke to the sound of light rain on my tent and decided that waiting out the weather might not be possible. I looked at my crampons and came to grips with the reality that I wouldn't get to summit the mountain by climbing on the glacier. I had hoped to tag along with a couple of other glacier climbers that had gotten camping permits for the same night. When I emerged from my shelter, though, I didn't see them anywhere. In fact, in my survey of the whole base camp area, I didn't see a single other tent.

I was alone.

As I packed and prayed in the rain, I let Nicole Mullen's voice blare from my phone. After tear down, I put her song, "Redeemer," on repeat. I splayed my arms out and slowly rotated to soak up the reality of the moment. With a voice that hadn't been used since lunchtime the previous day, I declared a list of things for which I was grateful at that moment. With a trembling voice, I tried to sing along. I wept until the water on my cheeks was warm.

They may have been tears of joy or gratitude or just a sense of smallness in light of a single, humbling mountain in a wilderness full of even less-approachable peaks. I felt grateful for the chance to have slept where I did. Candidly, I felt accomplished for being the only one to press into the altitude's wrath while others, I learned later, had hunkered down by the Subarus in the parking lot.

I may have been grieving the loss or postponement of a dream to climb a glacier. I also may have been grieving the loss of the epic vacation photos my ego wanted. After a summer of my Virginia friends filling my Facebook newsfeed with cliché shots from Atlantic Ocean beaches, I wanted some pictures nobody would have in their newsfeeds. I had come to Sahale for a personal adventure and got that. I just didn't get the magazine-quality photo my ego and insecurities craved. Hours of contemplation in the tent had already let me process how that unhealthy motivation had been too large a part of my drive up the mountain.

My counselor hasn't read this story yet, but she would concur sight unseen. Lindsey often sounds just short of exasperated with a line I've memorized now: "You put a *lot* of energy into what people think of you." Sometimes that sentence is a declaration, sometimes an exclamation, sometimes a question. But it's never been wrong. Too often I compensate for that insecurity with bravado that devolves into arrogance. It usually looks like me dropping unnecessary adventure tales or business stats into conversations as a way to impress people into thinking I'm worthy of respect. The aftertaste of those prideful moments ferments in my soul and tastes like the "calf fries" I tried on a dare in Fort Worth.

In various Native American languages *Sahale* means *falcon*, *overhead*, and *high place*. So, it makes sense that I would be confronted by my myopic perspective at 7,600 feet above sea level. Jesus said his thoughts are higher than ours. His valuation of us is higher than our own. He sees us as priests and priestesses, bearers of his light, heirs of heaven. For those who surrender their lives to him, we are children of the Most High God—offspring of the Infinite Force that created the cosmos.

I'm embarrassed to admit that I ignore what Jesus thinks of me. (Lindsey has reminded me of this multiple times.) He made all of us in his image, worthy of love. He doesn't use our vacation pictures or adventure stories to determine what he thinks of us. He doesn't check bank statements or credit scores. He doesn't count the number of children we do or don't have. He doesn't have castes determined by marital status.

There is nothing we can do to impress him.

Thankfully, we don't have to.

We can't earn his love—any of it, let alone more of it. His love isn't a currency. There's no system to be gamed.

I love the lyrics Chandler Moore sings about this truth in the song, "Jireh." The first three lines often grab my aching heart.

"I'll never be more loved than I am right now. Wasn't holding You up, So there's nothing I can do to let You down."

The Apostle John wrote about a woman whose conversion story emerged from this realization. Jesus engaged an outcast woman, a social misfit who didn't feel worthy to even do a menial task like carrying water with the other women in her village. Jesus fully knew her brokenness and didn't recoil. He saw her shame and held it with kindness and acceptance. When she ran back into her village, her message wasn't, "I've met the Messiah!" or "The Christ has come!" No, she energetically proclaimed, "I am fully known by the man I just met!" People in her town ran out because she said that with joy. After five failed marriages and a sixth one in the works, her community knew well she had spent years searching for but not finding the cure to the ache of her soul—and ours.

She had found what we all crave. We all want to be fully known. We just don't expect to be accepted with careful grace.

To different degrees, we're all scared that people won't like the real us. But Jesus sees us, knows us better than we know ourselves, and still wants to be close to us. I'm still working to wrap my brain around his heart. When I do feel that grace, it's in places where I feel small. I feel his pleasure and approval while hiking on a winding forest trail or crossing a remote wilderness. I've bumped into his extravagant love while strapped into a paraglider, a helicopter, or a float plane. I absorb that acceptance while listening to a circle of teammates pray or joining musical anthems led by friends on my church's stage.

I've even encountered that acceptance on a YMCA basketball court.

Just over a decade ago, I was learning how to play basketball. Yes: if you're doing the math, I was picking it up in my early thirties. A little late, I know. Three mornings a week, I played pickup ball with guys who worked at my church. These were cool dudes and athletes with years of practice. They knew what to do with the ball in seemingly every situation. I panicked a lot. I got a lot wrong, and I asked a lot of questions. I felt like an outsider or at least someone who needed to prove I deserved to be in that gym.

Then one morning, while walking off the court to head to our day jobs, Harney stopped me in my tracks with a message from Jesus. He looked me in the eyes to make sure I absorbed it. "Ryan, one of these days you're going to realize we like you for who you are." Those were life-giving words. I felt like the woman Jesus befriended at the well.

Sahale in Hindi means *trip*, and I've found that the absorption of Jesus' declarations looks more like an expedition than a lightning strike. It's not a light switch that stays on for me, but the flickers show me what can be—what I can be. So, I take a few steps forward for each step I go sideways or backward. I need regular infusions of Scripture, camaraderie, and wilderness. I need safe places like Lindsey's office and free spaces like the front row of chairs at my church on a Sunday morning.

I don't know your spiritual pathway, your Enneagram type, or how you best sense God's presence; but I hope you know what, where, and how you can absorb it. If not, search for it. When you experience that moment of transcendence, document it. Look for patterns or common denominators in how and why you got there. Thankfully, Jesus promises to be found when we search.

Our searching and knowing aren't just for us, though. When Jesus told us to take his good news to the world on his behalf, he wanted us to take that message with us. Love and acceptance came to us on their way to someone else. It came to Harney on its way to me. I sure hope someone else can say I've passed it onto them. Maybe that someone is you. If so, now it's your turn to let someone know their brokenness isn't beyond the love of Jesus. Their darkness isn't too black for his light. Their secrets aren't secrets, and the welcome is a standing offer anyway.

I need to hear that gospel everyday, multiple times a day. The more I hear it, the less I need those Facebook likes and the less often I find myself in a prison of trying too hard. Even those photogenic prisons that look like a rain-soaked tent on the edge of a cliff.

MOUNT NIMBUS

This will make a great story.

People ask me all the time what my favorite adventure has been. I don't have one. Somehow, ranking them cheapens the experiences. When I turn a critical eye to moments of exuberance or euphoria, it steals some of the joy and gratitude from the experience. The same holds true in terms of a favorite picture from my adventures. Multiple favorites take me back to equally incomparable moments.

One of my favorite shots, though, is a haphazard picture that I like better than the professional marketing images that drew me to the tour where I snapped the photo. Interestingly enough, this picture wasn't captured during an adrenaline-filled moment. I was taking a break, waiting on fellow adventurers in front of me to complete the next part of our single-file climb. The image doesn't showcase a conquering—a literal or figurative mountaintop experience. It doesn't show me in the sky, in big whitewater, or in a blurry race car. In fact, I'm not even in the picture.

I was standing on wet rock roughly 8,000 feet above sea level. Mist swirled around me and obscured the view of all the surrounding peaks, including the one I would soon summit. Clipped to a safety cable bolted to the mountain, I pulled out my phone to snap a quick shot of my fellow travelers ascending what I was about to climb.

As the clouds danced around us, I caught a glimpse of what I thought was the peak. Part of that assumption was based on my obscured view. Part of my expectation was rooted in the photos my tour company rightly uses in their marketing. The sunlit, blue sky images I saw on Instagram left the impression that this spire of rock in front of me was the peak. The tour operator's website added to that impression by showing one of their transport helicopters hovering in the background— not of the real peak but of this more iconic formation. Mount Nimbus' false summit in question is the pointiest peak I've ever seen in person. The granite spire rises with uneven, cragged edges that converge at the top for a surface area a little bigger than the front seat of your car. We each took turns at its pinnacle with one leg hanging down its north face and one leg dangling on its south side. On a clear day, this lone spire would have watched over the full day's tour. In the rain and wind, though, we didn't meet it until we got to the base of its last pitch.

Many of us had flown from the States or Eastern Canada just to conquer Mount Nimbus. We wanted the pictures, the videos, and the accomplishment it promised. (I was even wearing a backpack-mounted GoPro rig to mimic a chase drone.) It was cold on this second-to-last tour of the year before they shut down due to pending snow. Airborne moisture gathered on our red cheeks and atop our boots. Our rain gear added an audible crunch to all of our movements. Low visibility at scenic overlooks defeated some of the purpose of our challenge.

I could sense some frustration from others. A few minutes after I had put my phone back in my pocket, I heard my voice blurt to the doctor and the landscaper in front of me, "The more inclement the weather, the greater the sense of accomplishment." It wasn't manufactured Pollyanna sunshine. In my head I was seeing the dramatic documentary footage. I felt like an explorer, a *real* mountain climber in the cold rain. "We're getting better stories to tell," I added.

Almost all of the movies we love reveal the stories of people overcoming obstacles, challenges, or mysteries. The best stories include suspense or triumph, problems or misunderstandings. Most of the tales we retell from our own lives center on moments we didn't expect, hurdles we overcame, or frustrations we resolved. We like watching heroes surpass fate, and we want others to see the hero inside of us.

If you're like me, though, you don't like having that dramatic tension in real life, in current circumstances. Don't you just wish to get past the obstacle, past the discomfort, past the restlessness? When a relationship hits a chasm, I don't imagine the future narrative. When a massive bill comes in the mail, I don't think, "This is going to make the story better." When I'm facing overtime for months on end, I don't ponder how this stretch is providing the backdrop for the protagonist's character development. When I read stories of natural disasters, wonky political episodes, tragic human suffering, and racial injustice, I don't think about epic redemption.

I just want it all to end.

Soon, please?

I can't speak for you, but part of my frustration comes from comparing my situation to the marketing photos. Some days have gray skies instead of blue skies, slick rocks instead of grippy ones, myopic views instead of vast vistas. On some days, you can only hear the helicopter in the vague distance instead of it hovering for epic photos for your Instagram. *This isn't what I signed up for. I thought it would be different.* The tourist brochures tell us that cancer is only for old people. Betrayal is for movie summaries on IMDB. Hashtags imply that sexual molestation happens only to people we don't know and love. Sitcoms portray significant home repairs as punchlines in exaggerated physical comedies. Chronic pain, chemical addiction, and crippling financial debt are just statistical categories in BuzzFeed or *USA Today* articles. They're infographics, not personal illustrations. The untimely death or special needs of a child are supposed to comprise a tender chapter or two in a memoir, not be a reality for people in our nonfiction lives.

It wasn't supposed to be this way.

The unfairness and seeming randomness make the discomfort heavier. And it's not just the big things. I feel out of sorts when I get more than one Monday in a workweek, when the traffic signal has cycled twice without sensing my car at the white stripe, or when I get late-night texts from people asking questions. I relate to the exasperation of my wife the other day, when she blurted, "There's so many crises this week!"

A misconception our western culture brings to following Jesus is that being his friend or apprentice will make our lives easier. Jesus actually promised the opposite. I don't know about you, but that tempts me to go all Eeyore on life. The non-prosperity Gospel makes me want to write a second Ecclesiastes. *Woe is everyone.* As an alternative, I'm tempted to buoy my soul with comparisons to people who have it worse: the child slaves digging for my iPhone's precious metals, the parents who buried their school shooting victims, the women whose witch doctors have mutilated their physical femininity.

Neither of those responses is right or healthy. Jesus' brother gave us a different way to look at hardship. James wrote that trouble is an opportunity for joy because crises lead us to perseverance, and perseverance leads us to faith. We can't buy perseverance. We can't purchase faith or barter for it. If we want a life story that shows we followed Jesus, we actually need to follow Jesus; and he frequents hard places. Sure, he leads to green pastures where his burden is light; but he also walks through the valley of the shadow of death and asks God to let him not drink the cup of suffering.

We'll never have to drink a cup of anything as stout as what Jesus endured. That said, our cups can taste like fermented persimmons or laundry detergent—maybe both. That walk in Jesus' shadow bruises our feet. But—BUT—being close to Jesus feels supernatural. When we share in his mission and the ensuing hardships, we feel part of something bigger than ourselves, loved by something bigger than our respective hearts. At least I do. It's overwhelming.

When COVID-19 hit our economy, it whacked a huge dent in my business. Thankfully, it also gave me more time to play disc golf with my dear friend, Nate. Nora, his two-year-old daughter, joined us for most of those rounds and would regularly ask, "Uncle Ryan, can I hold you?" What Nora meant by those five words was actually a slightly different request. She wanted me to carry her, and almost every time she asked, I obliged. (Wouldn't you, if asked that way?) I also spent a lot of mornings playing disc golf alone in the woods or just walking mountain trails. By the end of the summer, I would blurt to Jesus through hot tears, "Can I hold you?"

I can't hold God. I can't touch Jesus. I couldn't tell you the color or smell or height of the Holy Spirit. I can't even hold the trees and rocks and clouds I do see.

"Can I hold you?"

Just like Nora, I wasn't really asking to be held. I was asking for my weight to be swept off my weary legs. I didn't know where Jesus would carry me. But like Nora, I knew we'd get closer to the equivalent of where she wanted to go at the park: to our cars in the parking lot, to our snacks next to our car seats, to baths and bedtime stories at our respective homes.

"Can I hold you?"

While listening to worshipful songs, I would raise my hands like Nora does for me to pick her up—until my face contorted into sobbing. One time, I had to stop walking because my vision was too blurred. But those were good tears from a cathartic release. They washed affirmation over me. Like more and more times over the past decade, I felt seen and heard. Rays of empathy shone through the trees along with the angular rays of dawn. I had to stop on several occasions and feel the rough bark of the trees, to dip my hands in tiny streams, to rub aromatic leaves in my hands and then dip my nose to my palm to absorb the smell. Heaven felt tangible. I can describe it only as a cosmic pleasure—first a sense of knowing that I did the right thing, the hard thing, the endurance thing, and then a sense of approval and affection.

It's as if the Author confirms that I've advanced the plot toward his desired ending.

The end of our story isn't the end of our lives. Our story lives longer than our legacy. Our faith can bear fruit well past our last breath. Even if our whole lives are difficult, resolution awaits. I don't mean that in a sweet-by-and-by kind of way. Our story is somehow woven with other stories. Our narratives affect those in other chapters, and we're all somehow part of an epic anthology. Our challenges, our obstacles, and our hardships create the tension where God reveals himself. Sometimes that's to and through us. At other times, it's to and through the authors writing beside us. It might just be that the promised perseverance and then faith we grow is not just our own but someone else's.

We're all on our way to a better life story. Well, we can be.

If you embrace the tension, you embrace the story. If you rustle a little further in your rain pants and lean forward under your heavy backpack, you advance the plot. If you feel the cold rain on your cheeks while the fog steals your photogenic accomplishment, you become a more intriguing character for those observing your faith. If you reach one step and then two out of your comfort zone, you just might find your faith has taken you beyond what you thought possible.

Maybe that progress does not include physical healing. Maybe that story still leaves you still financially bankrupt. Maybe that adventure still includes a vacancy where you hoped a spouse or children or employment would be. But maybe, just maybe, you'll find the reward that is knowing you were climbing the right mountain at the right time with the right people. If that happens while you're following Jesus, I hope you get lots of chances to tell those stories—his stories—over and over again.

THE CHASE

Jesus often hides in plain sight.

My first trip to Western Norway ambushed me. I was alone there while my wife shepherded a team at a prostitute rescue organization in Managua, Nicaragua. Multiple times on that first Norway trip, I got choked up while looking at my natural surroundings with evocative music in my headphones. My heart felt overwhelmed in solitude. In rugged, rocky surroundings, a softness crushed me. I don't know what I was hoping to find in Norway that first time, but I found what many kings could not.

More on that in a second.

I've explored around two dozen countries, but Norway introduced me to unprecedented views. "Beautiful" falls short. "Impressive" understates. "Pristine" might work if it hadn't been cheapened by so many marketers.

The bus-and-ferry tour operator marketed my only guided day as "The Royal Fjord Tour." Apparently, before photography was invented, European royalty sailed into these fjords to see them in person. For probably a couple hundred years, the experience I was absorbing was that kind of vacation luxury.

Norwegian engineers have since created incredible infrastructure for exploring the lush, inhospitable place. You can tell that less than a century's worth of human history has enjoyed its current access to the fjords and islands. Now, unlike in the olden days, tourists outnumber locals in plenty of spots. Before all of the two-lane roads, tunnels, bridges, and ferries, only weathered sailors and intrepid homesteaders absorbed these hidden corners on a regular basis. I can't imagine the hardship they endured to get there.

I wanted to pinch myself for the exclusivity, even though there were dozens of people at one stop and hundreds at another. What had been hidden for millennia and arduous for centuries came at the end of a few keystrokes and mouse clicks for me. It took me a single day to get there—from another continent. Three minutes after shivering in the morning cold, I could grab a hot cocoa. When the afternoon grew warm, I could retreat to air conditioning. The richest, most powerful kings of the past had these fjords to themselves, but they couldn't have enjoyed many of the luxuries I'm tempted to take for granted.

After the fjord tour, I drove a rental car up and over a one-lane bridge onto Runde Island—to lodge overnight in a former lighthouse keeper's cabin. As I walked back to my bedroom from the far point of the island, a tiny wildflower stopped me in my tracks. From cracks in a house-sized boulder, its pink petals trembled under the breath of the North Sea. I wondered in how many remote places on the planet Jesus had planted these fragile flowers. How many of those locations have not yet been visited by human eyes and feet? My memory flashed to the previous August and the flowers I saw growing out of the rock cliffs next to the Conrad Glacier in Western Canada—stone faces that had been covered by ice until just five years prior to my visit.

As I reflected on that flower in the lighthouse's rocks, I heard a whisper, a reminder of a verse I've read dozens of times. 3,000 years ago, a Hebrew scribe wrote, "It is the glory of God to conceal a matter, but the glory of kings is to search out a matter." That verse had puzzled me for decades until that trip to Norway.

Jesus makes beautiful things for himself, whether we will ever find them. He paints and sculpts because he can, because he enjoys it. He creates beauty just to store it—if only for a season. He curates gardens and fountains where we can't take credit for them. He confounds scientists with symbiotic species that couldn't have evolved separately or even together. He explodes biodiversity beyond pragmatism. He fills the world with enigmas and paradoxes and mysteries. And he has done this for millennia, knowing that we would take centuries to find his masterpieces—that we might never find them.

I was struck that these far-flung discoveries have been my destiny. My name, Ryan, came to the English language by way of the Latin *Rex* (from which my Spanish-speaking friends get their *Rey*). It means "little king." The roots of my family name, George, dig down to origins of "in the earth" or "works in the dirt." So, I was meant to either (A) lead a bunch of farmers and excavators or (B) be one who searches out God's secrets around the world.

I'll take "THE SECOND ONE" for $800, Alex.

We live in an amazing time. Relative to human history, we're all kings. Even if we all can't jump on planes to the corners of the map, we can all afford to explore Google Images and Instagram. With a few clicks or taps, we can look into the cosmos or into microscopic cells. For the last half decade, every time I open a new Chrome window on my office iMac, a Google Earth plug-in populates my monitor with a striking aerial image. These natural wonders have become so commonplace, that I rarely linger on them anymore. That's because awe leaks, and wonder fades. I sometimes scroll through gorgeous Instagram images like I'm spinning the big Showcase Showdown wheel on *The Price is Right*. I grow numb to splendor. *Yawn. I've seen fifty other shots like this.*

I fight that apathy with travel. The intentionality of that worship influences my destinations; I pursue feeling small and even insignificant. That headspace is also why I have a "Desert Devotions" playlist on my phone and a set of headphones in every backpack. Solomon was very right. I take glory in my Lilliputian conquering, my tourist version of exploring. Ironically, though, that pursuit leads me back to the glory that can never be mine.

That is why God displays these wonders out in the wide open. He knows vastness will slow our approach. That's also why he shrouds his art within roughly hewn citadels. He wants native sounds to drown out our cares when we discover his pervasive creativity. He wants to see our eyes widen, to watch our jaws drop, to hear those involuntary exhales. He takes pleasure in our pursuit of glory leading us to his. Despite the equipment and technology humankind has amassed, the psalmist's claims are still true with lines like, "His greatness is unsearchable," and, "No man can measure his greatness."

For hundreds of years, Norway has held to *allemannsrett*, which translates to English as "everyman's right." Basically, it means that anyone—Norwegian or not—has the right to hike and camp on public lands and at least 150 meters from buildings on private land. The former king of Norway invited everyone to explore the beauties of his kingdom, and that spirit has lived on for centuries.

But Norwegian royalty was late to the game. Jesus had already invited everyone on the planet to explore his domain. He wanted— and still wants—us to discover his beauty, his serendipity, and his creativity. Since we entered his planet, he wanted to use it to reveal his character and our need for it. For thousands of years, he has welcomed us into spiritual expeditions too. He can show off his God-ness in nature and relationships and introspection. He can reveal his heart for us and all people in both the tiny details of a leaf and the impressive heft of a glacier.

To encourage more exploration, he promised that those who seek him will find him. I claim that promise almost every time I leave civilization. You can too. We don't need a passport to realize this, though. We don't need hiking boots or wetsuits, either. Because God lives everywhere, his sovereign omnipotence wiggles out of the cracks of our daily lives. He stores eternal moments at the grocery store, in the passenger seat of your minivan, and even in office cubicles. He reveals a piece of himself at your local playground and bike path. He waits for you to find part of his character in your garden and in your garage. He's scheduled whispers to your heart around a campfire with his other kids and in a passage of Scripture you've read a dozen times. He's embargoed your next discovery for when you're in a canoe or in the car listening to a podcast. He has divine encounters planned in backcountry campsites and in church parking lots.

He can and will be found by those who intentionally explore his kingdom, his presence, and his transcribed words.

That promise only works, though, when we hold up our end of the deal. We must seek what Sovereignty stores in far places. We must keep our eyes open and our feet moving. We must go further than the kings who went before us. We can't settle for what we already know of Jesus. He's left a lot more out there for us to find and realize and fully know. We are royal heirs to his kingdom. We are little kings and queens assigned to this journey of discovery. If we want more of Jesus—if we want to know him better—his revelation is waiting for us.

And it might just be hiding in plain sight.

THE END OF THE WORLD

Faith requires uncomfortable mystery.

I don't fault the people who misnamed the bottom tip of South America. The folks who branded *Fin Del Mundo* lived in simpler times with simpler ignorance. Explorers and cartographers—not satellites and software—drew their maps.

My ship to Antarctica, the *M/V Ortelius*, bore the name of the first man to create a world atlas. Amazingly, he even included drawings of the seventh continent. I met this former Russian research vessel in Ushuaia ("oo-SHWĪ-uh"), Argentina. There isn't much to do down by the port other than walk the streets or wharf parks. The cold city juxtaposes opposing impressions. The buildings, sidewalks, and roads flow disheveled down to the Beagle Channel; but the stores and pedestrians are wrapped in expensive, fashionable apparel. Locals who can't speak English work in stores whose crackling speakers play Jack Johnson, Ed Sheeran, and Beyoncé. Gourmet restaurant aromas swirl with the fumes of the diesel engines of cars not safe enough to be sold in the States.

I lost count of the signs, buildings, and cars there labeled with the local slogan: *El Fin Del Mundo*. If it's been a few years since Spanish class, that phrase translates into English as "End of the World." When you hear "end of the world," you probably imagine some post-apocalyptic wasteland. For me, that phrase evokes less a place and more a way of life, a view of the future. It's a feeble existence until there is no more existence. But the end of the world is a physical place—and not just to members of the Flat Earth Society. For decades or maybe a couple of centuries, this outpost owned global consensus as the last piece of land before, well, before no man's land or no land at all. Ushuaia still holds the distinction of the southernmost city on the planet. My Uncle Steve now owns a Hard Rock Cafe shirt that celebrates that.

I find irony in *El Fin Del Mundo*, though, since the main attraction there is the port. The place once considered the end of it all huddles around the docks where tourists grab ships to other destinations. It wasn't the beginning of any of our journeys, but it wasn't the end, either. This city, wedged between a mountain and the sea, functions like a vault for a gymnast. Momentum builds to this sliver of a city and then unleashes your kinetic energy, propelling you into the yet-unknown. It might be the end of a run, but it's also the launch pad to realization and accomplishment. If it's the end of the world, it's also the beginning of a new one.

I was struck by the notion inherent in this misnamed geography: our seeming end of the world is often the gateway to God's grand adventures.

The end of the world looms like a shadow in the margins around the stories that fill our screens. The news is filled with pre-apocalyptic sorrows and precursors to dystopia. Even without world news, pain and heartbreak are running rampant amongst my friends and their friends. Probably yours too. I don't know about you, but unfaithful spouses, cancerous organs, sexual abuse, joblessness, mental illness, and slavery to debt are devouring people I care about. The end of the world shadows over their hearts and their perspective.

One by one, though, I've seen God leverage this pain for his glory and his redemptive story. Those crucibles have yielded the fruit of sovereign camaraderie, authentic worship, and even restorative ministry. Tears still fall, but they have watered the fertile soil of the soul. Friends and loved ones have found that the end of the world is just the end of the land they're leaving. They are embarking on new journeys. Like me in Ushuaia, they haven't known exactly what's in store for them—right before it gets awesome.

I'm not talking TV-evangelist awesome with six-figure cars and seven-figure houses. Nobody sprinkled holy water on their hospital bills and then found Benjamins in their refrigerator. Please don't hear that they necessarily beat disease, betrayal, or loneliness—even though some did. This isn't Pollyanna rebranding her challenges, either. Silver linings by definition frame larger, darker clouds.

In crushing hardships, we've found clarity and sufficiency and encouragement. We've witnessed mercy and serendipity and omniscience. We've felt affection and affirmation and a surreal presence of something or Someone bigger than us. We've felt connected in the way every human craves. Goodbyes still hurt. Losses still stung. Tears still fell. But that pain wasn't wasted. Tragedy, disappointment, and betrayal found meaning.

The overwhelming truths we find in hardship matter. I wouldn't want to relive some of the moments and seasons I've endured, but I also wouldn't trade how my dependence on Sovereignty has let me feel the heartbeat of Jesus as if through a stethoscope.

My editor wants me to tell you stories here—to prove this isn't hyperbole or cliché, to make this concept practical. There aren't steps to these moments, though—at least not any codified or choreographed. I don't know if I could tease out a pattern, but I can point to mile marker experiences on the path behind me.

I remember watching a mother worshipping on the front row of our sanctuary, hands raised and open—at the memorial service for her son. The twenty-something youth leader had died not long after his honeymoon in a tragic accident. Kendall's death contributed to his dad's painful but beautiful spiritual reformation, and that dad stepped into my life when my father made choices to step out of mine. I will never forget the inscription of the book Bob gave me to explain his journey to see the goodness of Jesus' heart: "You remind me of my son." I was overwhelmed when I read those words. I still am. I now know my heavenly father's heart better because an earthly father lost his son.

I won't ever forget the night one of my closest friends, Aaron, told our prayer group he didn't feel like discussing a Bible passage with the rest of the circle because he was too blinded by the fresh loss of his unborn child. As someone who had actively avoided parenthood, I felt unworthy to pray for him and offered to pray last. I looked up from the floor and asked Nate, whose wife had recently lost back-to-back pregnancies, to start our prayer over him. Those losses drew our hearts together and aligned our hearts with a longing Father. Both of those men now dote on daughters birthed from rainbows. Nate lets me carry both of his precious girls in my arms—sometimes at the same time.

Aaron's oldest daughter runs into my arms every Sunday morning in my church's parking lot, and his youngest is one of the only people in the world I don't mind calling me "Ry."

Both Nate and Aaron have walked in the woods with me, prayed with me, and coached me through the adventure that has been the unplanned fatherhood of a teenage daughter. (I became a dad at forty-one years old while I was on a helicopter expedition with Aaron in British Columbia. When we got back to civilization, I read a text message that explained how a fifteen-year-old girl had come to live first in our guest bedroom back in Virginia.) I have the courage to lean into something I had avoided if only to honor the longing my friends had for the opportunity.

I once torched a bridge to a mentor, but he refused to let it burn. A few days after I went nuclear in his email inbox, Dave didn't just forgive me. He invited me to ride with him in his ultralight. I had hurt his heart, but he welcomed me into his passion. The seats in a tandem ultralight, which is basically a powered hang glider, require physical proximity similar to that of riding a motorcycle. Have you ever sat that close to someone after hurting them? I now have.

That moment took me back to when our knees were the same distance apart at the funeral of a friend who had died of a heart attack while flying *his* ultralight. Dave found me on the back row, sat next to me, draped his arm over my sagging shoulders, and poured empathy into my soul. A friend had died, but a friendship with eternal consequences blossomed. Dave taught me how a follower of Jesus sits with the hurting and those who hurt you. That gesture prepared me for moments to sit with those who'd lost their jobs, their marriages, their innocence, and their dreams.

After finally paying off approximately $70,000 of surprise

construction costs that arrived after closing on our new house, I was handed a foundation repair bill of more than $10,000. The contractor got counsel that his insurance would cover it, and I could easily trigger his policy coverage if I sued his company. One problem: we attended the same church. We took the situation to our elders, who asked us not to use the court system for remedy. They asked us to pray together once a week for five weeks and incorporate some sort of daily individual prayer practice centered on the situation. At the end of the five weeks, if God hadn't provided the money for either of us, the church offered to pay the bill. My builder and I met atop Candlers Mountain each week to pray, and I journaled daily prayers for the first time in my life. At the second elders meeting, I wept while reading from my journal and absolved the builder and the church of any financial responsibility.

I ate the bill. That meant I had to postpone some of my plans and dreams, but the Gospel grew expensive and precious in my heart over those five weeks of prayer. The mission of the global church became more rooted in my soul. My connection to and respect for the souls that guide my local assembly blossomed. I lost almost $11,000 but gained a new kind of perseverance and a very real sense of Jesus' affirmation.

In his fantastic book, *God of the Pandemic*, N.T. Wright points out that at least part of the famous promise that God works everything out for the good of his saints is that he brings the beautiful wholeness of heaven to a broken world *through* his saints. That's Advent. And the spiritual adventure through which it often arrives is not an exercise to whitewash pain or put a bow on hardship. No. It's to leverage temporal trials for eternal advancement—not just for an ethereal future but in *Los Fines del Mundo* of our daily lives. The grandest adventures require perseverance against stout resistance. Humanity's greatest physical achievements have been birthed from hunger and thirst, pain and even death. The end of many explorers' worlds has added lines to maps that guided others to new territory.

The moments of the unknown, the undone, and the unfair are right where God often reveals his character, where he joins us. Immanuel, God with us. Some of the most intimate encounters I've had with The Creator of the Universe have come when I felt most uncertain, most out of control. At the end of my confidence, my knowledge, and my ability is where he was waiting. And I should've known that in advance, because faith starts when we go further than the last firm ground we've known.

I'm writing these paragraphs as one who has literally stood upon *El Fin del Mundo*. I'm here to tell you the end of the world—or at least our worlds—is not what you or I think it is. First, wherever you and I find ourselves is not the end. Our story isn't over, even if we never spend another conscious second on this planet. We are written into a grander story with eternal implications. Second, at our respective *Los Fines del Mundo* stand the gateways to beautiful progress. Based on my experience and that of my friends, I anticipate the southernmost ports of our lives hold the ships to some incredible adventures.

There's more in store. There's more capital-L life. There's more newness. There's more Immanuel. There are more stories, more missions, and more sovereign assignments. There are more moments in the "valley of the shadow of death" and even more promises of "I am with you." No matter how much we know, there's even more we don't know—that we can know. For all of the times when "all is lost," we can also discover what it means to be found and known and loved. At the end of the world, as we know it, waits a world we don't yet know has been our destiny.

WINDOW STICKERS

Humility feels like ripping off a hundred Band-Aids.

For a handful of summers, I attended a conference where the host always prefaced the diverse speaker lineup with, "If you're humble enough, you can learn from anyone." I've always liked that. I love learning new things. I absorb so many TED talks, nonfiction books, and science podcasts, that I'm about to start taking them intravenously. The hard part for me has always been the "humble enough" requirement.

Early in my travels, G.K. Chesterton confronted my myopic mind. "The whole object of travel is not to set foot on foreign land; it is, at last, to set foot on one's own country as a foreign land." This transition that Chesterton recommends happens best when I'm "humble enough," when I welcome revelation through humility.

I love where I live. I love why it's home. But I've gradually allowed the rest of the world to own pieces of my soul. I've let my heart feel at home in places I didn't even know existed even a decade ago. While I still default to pizza when eating abroad, I've made sure to carry a lot of curiosity with me and to pack less judgment.

That curiosity led to a personal revelation in Argentina. On my way to Antarctica, I spent a Thanksgiving evening in the bustling metropolis of Buenos Aires and a Black Friday in the sleepy port town of Ushuaia. In both places, I noticed large, white, oval stickers on the rear windows of vehicles in surrounding traffic. Each held a black numeral ending in zero. The numbers varied from one vehicle to the next, ranging from 80 to 110. Most of the numbers appeared on what looked to be commercial vehicles. *Was it a weight rating?* Nope. The numbers seemed inversely proportional to the size of the truck or van. *Did it indicate some sort of tire rating? A classification of cargo?*

After burning through guesses, I asked a taxi driver what they meant. Turns out, they're the maximum speed limit in kilometers per hour for that specific vehicle. Even if the posted speed limit were higher than what was shown on the sticker, the speed noted on the sticker was as fast as the driver could legally drive that vehicle.

My first thought was that I'm thankful we don't have these in the States—especially on my MINI. That would be brutal! The next thing that popped into my head was a bit more metaphorical: *How many of us move around in life with virtual stickers announcing our limitations?*

And then, *What are my stickers?*

Candidly, my top-left window is crowded with more than one stated limit. One sticker says UNATTRACTIVE. It's jammed between the one that says ANNOYING and the one that reads IMMATURE. The cascade continues with UNCOORDINATED and even HYPOCRITE.

Drivers behind me in life's traffic can clearly tell that the cool kids don't sit at my lunch table. I waver between feeling not enough of something for peers and too much of something for others. And I assume everybody knows I'm both trying too hard and not trying enough.

So, I drive my inadequate self—as fast as I'm allowed—to parking spots that might distract from my stickers. I head to the fraternity of servants in my church's parking lot, to remote lighthouses along the coast of Norway, and even out onto the wings of a biplane while it's pulling aerobatic maneuvers. I parallel park behind Facebook or back into garage spots on Instagram. With some hashtags and sleight of hand media, I invite others to stand in front of my vehicle or beside it. I hope you and everybody else see the other, stickerless windows and that you're distracted by my colorful advertising on the door. I hope I'm the only one who sees my stickers, but deep down I feel that everyone stares at them—and that the stickers comprise everyone's first or lasting impression of me.

As I'm writing this, I know that assumption is preposterous; but I don't *live* like it's preposterous. Maybe you can relate. Your stickers have different words in them—a word an angry parent yelled, a label a bully gave you, or the opposite of a compliment you've waited your whole life to hear.

I used to think the solution for all of us was to cover those stickers with positive affirmations or things we want people to associate with us. Years ago, I used a service called Klout to recommend content to share on social media. I fell in love with their slogan, "Be known for what you love." *What if we all just told the world what we loved?*

"Be known for what you love" became a mantra for me. I worked hard on social media not to post critical content but to focus on what excites me. I labored over captions to tell people stories of the lessons and introspections of my adventures. I pulled back the curtain on internal struggles to balance the not-so-humble bragging inherent in my photos and videos. I encouraged other people to chase physical and spiritual adventures.

I diligently crafted new stickers, improved labels.

The problem was the adhesive. It didn't last like the glue on my limits. I had to keep adventuring, keep capturing, and keep relabeling. Thankfully, I enjoy both chasing adventure and telling stories; but as my therapist often tells me, "That sounds like a lot of work!"

Since the Garden of Eden, we've all been pulling virtual fig leaves over our vulnerabilities. Sewing leaves is not easy. Making leafy garments stylish proves downright impossible. Maybe that's why stress and anxiety keep swallowing more and more of us. We're the most medicated and entertained generation in human history, and collectively we still can't sleep at night. Contentedness seems farther away than ever. Our online connectedness has raised the stakes for what goes in those white ovals. We want the hundreds, thousands, or even millions of people in our audience to see only the stickers we want to be read.

I know I've written this a lot, but Jesus told us that he came to bring us life. The process of transferring that life to us requires him to peel off those old stickers. He didn't assign those words. He doesn't believe their lies. The first-century eyewitnesses who wrote his biographies let us know Jesus labels us with words like *beloved* and *chosen* and *royal*. We didn't earn those words. We can't buy those stickers. When we surrender our wills and our striving, we receive those stickers as gifts.

That doesn't mean removing the old stickers is easy. Pulling nostril hair out with wax strips hurts less than peeling these stickers off. Band-Aids feel like sticky notes in comparison. Unless you're superhuman, you'll probably need outside help to scrape them off your glass. I'm not sure how it works for others, but the process Jesus is using in my life requires awkward conversations. People who love Jesus drop hard truths on me and ask me harder questions. When Jesus has called my name in the cool of the morning, I've had to walk naked out from behind both convenient bushes and the topiary I've tended for decades. That walk regularly brings a cringe to my face and a pang in my soul.

That discomfort has sometimes driven me to attempt a different strategy. When I've tried to prove my insecurities wrong, I've compensated with accomplishment and self-importance (emphasis on *tried*). It usually doesn't end well. I typically just prove the adage: "The path to humility is through humiliation."

Almost every sand castle I've built has toppled, often in an ironic fashion—seemingly for emphasis. Each fake medal I've won has left green circles on my shirt. And I've learned with regret that when I feel admirable, that sense of being enough has often come at the expense of someone else feeling less than enough.

Instead of being confident in what Jesus declares to be my reality, I've played the role of a public relations firm: selling a narrative to change the public's perception. *Just give me a chance to prove myself. You'll see.* I crave a meritocracy or at least the perception of it. When I find one, I figure out which competitions match my skillset and then go all Peyton Manning on my preparation. I get good enough to take pride in an area of my life and, in so doing, drive my sticker-plastered car into the ditch on the other side of the self-esteem road.

Insecurity and pride comprise two sides of the same coin. Both focus on the valuation of someone other than Jesus. For us to conquer either insecurity or pride, we need to constantly remind ourselves that others don't determine our value. Nobody but Jesus chooses our stickers. And that *nobody* includes us. *Jesus* named us. *Jesus* wrapped us in labels only he could earn. *Jesus* chose those labels for us "before the foundation of the world."

That's where I am on the journey now: continually absorbing reminders of where my value originates. That requires reading sacred passages, listening to truth-laden songs, meeting with a therapist, and journaling my blessings. Oh, and something maybe a bit counterintuitive: I've fully embraced the ancient proverb, "If you want to learn, teach." I've made a daily habit of writing, texting, or speaking encouragements to my friends. I get healthier when I focus on reminding others what labels Jesus gave them. Jesus shows up in those moments to whisper, "That's true of you too."

That's no accident. Jesus assigned our calling before we were born—to glorify him. So, our truest self and our real identity blossom when we're glory *givers*, not glory *earners*. When we're pouring our energy and resources into his kingdom, he rewards us with a sense of his presence and pleasure. When we pursue his reputation instead of our own, he gifts us with moments of transcendence. We get goosebumps from being at the right place at the right time. We feel a sense of how our little lives fit into an infinite matrix. Eternity buzzes in our hearts.

When we're focused on his stickers, we're less concerned about our own.

I know: that sounds like a Sunday school answer. I get it if that sentence makes you roll your eyes. If the church in the past has handed you insufficient Band-Aids, glib clichés, and shallow dismissals, that might reverberate like a claim of a spiritual snake oil salesman. But I've lived it. I've felt life pulse through me from adrenaline, but I've felt capital-L life pulse through me from supernatural encounters. Bungee jumping, wing walking, and whitewater kayaking momentarily cover my insecurities. Driving a racecar, hanging off a cliff, and paragliding off a mountain fill me with confidence, especially after I post the evidence online. But those spiritual moments . . . man! That's when I feel fully alive. I'm not worried about what others think. I don't need social media to know. I'm unaware of any stickers on my car.

When I'm "humble enough," my home of insecurities seems foreign, and I get excited to travel back out into a new and exciting world. I lose myself while exploring an upside-down kingdom, a place that makes sense only after I've spent enough time there to forget what right-side up felt like.

NO SPEEDOMETER

Stay five car lengths behind Jesus.

Don't die! Don't die! Don't die!

Self-talk is probably supposed to sound more affirming than that, but those six words hijacked my brain as I fought turn one at Charlotte Motor Speedway.

The world blurred past me, somehow quiet enough for those six words to be louder than the frenzy around me. It was as if I couldn't hear the thunder of my exhaust. Those raspy decibels had mesmerized me when I first drove out of the tunnel and onto the infield. Now wedged into a fiberglass cockpit, I didn't hear the tires on the asphalt or the violently shaking chassis. The empty stands could've held their 100,000 screaming fans, and I wouldn't have noticed them, either.

The voice inside my head was deafening.

An hour earlier, inside the racing school classroom, the instructor had asked like a professional wrestling emcee, "Who's going to drive the fastest!?" A bunch of middle-aged men in cargo shorts and golf shirts cheered. A decade younger than my classmates, I did not hoot or holler. I had just come from a slow preview lap of the track. The instructor had parked our van on that same *Don't die!* Turn—turn one. The slope was so steep, when I looked across from the front passenger seat and out his driver's side window, I saw nothing but asphalt. He diverted my gaze out the windshield. "See those white marks down in the corners?" I nodded. "That's where you're aiming. That's where your line is."

See, what I was about to experience wasn't a ride-along. We would be driving retired IndyCar racecars, and they held only one seat. We didn't get a few laps first with an instructor driving. We were on our own. With only a few laps in the total experience, we couldn't afford practice loops. No, this would be open-wheel racing. We rookies had to memorize all of these marks and anticipate them coming off the straightaways.

Back indoors, our teacher clarified that we might encounter times when we should abandon those white triangle cues. Our on-track instructors would be driving right in front of us, looking out their rearview mirrors almost the whole time. If they determined those lines were temporarily not ideal, we were to follow their lead no matter where they went.

Oh, and we had to stay five car lengths behind them. If we lagged any further back, our guides would slow down with the assumption that we couldn't handle their speed. If we encroached too close, they would throttle down to get us to return to a safe speed and distance.

"There are no speedometers in your cars. We want you to focus on your instructor. Also, we want you to have a good time. If you're constantly getting too close or too far back, it creates an accordion effect; and you won't get to fully enjoy your laps."

Our bona fide former racehorses had interiors as sparse as a go-kart. With some contorting, I squeezed my shoulders into the cockpit. Then the pit crew buckled my five-point harness and attached the steering wheel. In the pros, that wheel costs tens of thousands of dollars and includes all kinds of digital gauges as well as paddle shifters. My steering wheel looked like one of those generic chrome ones hanging from the wall at AutoZone.

A few minutes later, an ATV pushed me to a rolling start; I popped the clutch; and I followed a man I had never met out into a dozen circuits of North Carolina asphalt. Each lap seemed just a few seconds long. I rarely breathed other than in the straightaways.

After we pitted, I untangled myself from the straps, unfolded my still-buzzing joints, and stumbled out of the car. I looked up at the leaderboard, where our top speeds flickered from tiny orange bulbs. The giant Lite Brite pegs told me I had topped out in the low 140s—far below the rest of my class and well short of the 165 miles per hour teased as the potential top speed on the course's website.

Serendipitously, the organizers had miscounted my laps. As an apology, they offered me free laps after everyone else finished. As the cooler air of dinnertime approached, I twisted into the cockpit of a metallic-silver beast. I steeled myself—dared myself—to push faster. I recalled the teacher saying that the driver in front of me would go faster if he felt I was handling myself well at the current speed while staying those magical five car lengths from the brake light of his lead car.

After the first lap, the instructor seemed to be gradually accelerating;

but I couldn't tell by how much. It felt like ten miles an hour faster than my first laps. Maybe fifteen?

I got distracted from my calculations when I noticed my lead driver drift up closer to the fence. As we got to the back straightaway, I could see the NASCAR school's lead driver and his student on the inside lane where I had been driving. Their brochure and website had promised much lower top speeds, and their early laps proved slower still. We blew right past them but didn't dive back down into the turns after passing. No. We would be staying high side.

That's right: the rest of my laps screamed up next to the safety fence around the top of the track. I quickly grasped the reason those white marks had been painted down on the inside of the turns. Up on top, you don't hold the steering wheel. You fight it. You wrestle it. It's trying to yank out of your grip like a defiant preschooler or frantic piglet. This discovery hit me while entering turn one. That's when all thoughts left, except, *Don't die! Don't die! Don't die!*

I imagined that steering wheel whipping loose and my front right wheel slamming into the wall. I gritted my teeth and fought both centrifugal force and my cowardice to stay those five car lengths from the spoiler in front of me. On the straight stretches, I kept hoping the lead driver would go faster and let me redeem my low scores from the first round.

He wouldn't.

Alas, the white flag unfurled; and we coasted into the pits. Every body chemical that is supposed to surge in a fight-or-flight moment was pulsing with the vibration of my crackling racecar. I had gotten almost a dozen laps more than anyone else, but the time still seemed as disappointedly short as one of those coin-operated fire truck rides in the mall food court.

I removed my helmet and walked to the scoreboard. I wanted to bang my helmet on the concrete in frustration for not getting to discover what

I could handle out on the asphalt. I refrained because those helmets are expensive, and I didn't want to seem ungrateful for the school's generosity. As I approached the pit wall in my fire-retardant suit, I squinted at the bottom of the scoreboard. That's where I'd probably find my car number and my top speed. About halfway up from the bottom, I figured I must not have even made the leader board. For some reason, I kept reading up the list. To my surprise, my car number glowed second from the top—only half a mile per hour slower than the top scorer.

185.38

I had driven twenty miles an hour faster than the school had advertised. I had done so with no idea of this reality, no concept of how much more the fence had blurred. Then a thought hit me. *He probably wasn't legally allowed to take me any faster!* Satisfaction cracked my face into a grin. That grin pushed my cheeks higher until a smile erupted on my face. I pumped my fist or my helmet—or maybe my fist *and* my helmet. I had squeezed everything out of the experience I had hoped for and then some.

My ride home to Virginia looked very different. No blurred fences. No jiggling helmet. No deafening engine. Because I drive an old MINI Cooper, a massive speedometer stared back at me for more than three hours. Throughout my sixteen years of driving a MINI, I've often been annoyed that the speedometer wasn't right behind the steering wheel like a normal car. Instead, it's in the center of my dashboard, easily read by anyone sitting anywhere in my car.

It's ironic that I don't like others knowing how fast I'm driving, seeing as I quietly want my more public gauges in life to be out in front of everyone. I want friends and strangers alike to see how many people follow me, how many likes my social media posts achieve, how much my business is growing, and how many awards my work wins. I hope others notice my generosity, my vacation spots, and my ministry contributions. *See? I'm a great brother and uncle. I'm a good friend and congregant.*

I have often felt like I couldn't archive a good memory or verify a good life without digital proof—an online speedometer. The ironic reality is that some of the most fulfilling moments of my life have come in private encounters far from cameras and hundreds of miles from likes, comments, and shares. The legacy stuff usually happens offline. There's no infographic or Facebook emoji for the moments when I learn that I made a difference, that my contribution mattered. My ego is stroked by clicks, but my soul is assured when I see others benefit from our relationship or my surrender—or both. Influence feels better than affirmation.

As the creator of Veggie Tales and multiple other programs for children, Phil Vischer has spent a career making biblical concepts relatable to kids. He explained this dynamic well. He says, "Our impact doesn't occur when we pursue impact. Our impact occurs when we pursue God." In other words, all we have to do with this life is stay five car lengths behind our Instructor. If he moves toward less comfortable places, follow anyway. When it doesn't seem like he's doing what his promotional materials promised, follow anyway. When we feel like he doesn't recognize our goal, follow anyway.

When you want Jesus to move faster or resolve sooner, stay close; but don't push. When the only thing you seem able to do is hold on and not die, hold on. When holding on feels more like wrestling than steering, wrestle on. When life's happening so fast you can't remember what lap you're on, live on. When all you hear is deafening noise, and your world is shaking violently, look for the marks on the track that Jesus left for you.

Reread the verses you've highlighted in your Bible. Find your journal entries from when you remember hearing God's voice more clearly. Replay the songs that take you back to watershed spiritual moments. Ask your best friend or mentor out to coffee or for a hike, and ask them to pray truth over you.

When you're tempted to check a leader board, look to your leader instead. When you don't chase numbers and compliments, you just might get to experience abundantly more than you'd hoped or asked.

BEAR BAIT

Shoot high to avoid friendly fire.

I heard a .357 magnum hit the wood floor. I couldn't see it, but I knew the source of the thud.

I didn't know if its barrel was pointed at me. What I did know is that Jack's sleeping bag had blown a zipper. We both knew it was bone-chilling cold in our Appalachian Trail shelter. You don't need a thermometer or an app to tell you that. An app would've been nice, though. Neither of us anticipated the snow that would fall while we slept and eventually extinguish the coals that had warmed our long conversation after dinner. The air would drop below freezing, and Jack had no way to keep that air from pouring into what was now a folded blanket, a Jack taco.

To at least keep some wind off him, I erected my Bivy tent across the opening of the shelter. Our buddy, Aaron, erected his tent perpendicular to mine to frame Jack in. Aaron pulled his huge Labrador retriever into his tent, so Cinnamon wouldn't bark at small game during the night. Well, small game and bears. See, this section of the East Coast's longest trail is known for its black bear population. We hadn't seen any while foraging for firewood, but we hadn't broken out our mac' n' cheese or chicken alfredo dinners at that point. That's where Jack's .357 came in. To stop a bear at close range in the middle of the night, someone's going to need something other than bear spray or a pocket pistol.

When I heard that solid clunk, I told Jack, "Shoot high. I'll be the one on the bottom."

I didn't realize at the time how this flippant joke would become one of the key sentences of my life. I think about this story almost every time a disagreement or argument with my wife turns into a fight. I recall this request when I read headlines of racial tension, political corruption, and international conflict. This line comes back to me when I hear stories of abuse, neglect, and trafficking.

See, the Apostle Paul told his old friends that we don't wrestle with other humans. We fight invisible rulers, dark forces, and evil spirits. The language Paul uses leaves an impression that this is happening above us without us being able to see it. I know that sounds like a fairy tale, a horror movie, or a video game "rated M for mature." If you don't follow Jesus, weird suggestions like this probably don't help the Bible's believability. If you do follow Jesus, you've probably been weirded out when someone blames a normal human occurrence as "spiritual warfare."

"So, let me get this straight, Karen. Satan spilled your coffee?"

"Yes! It spilled onto my 'Not today, Satan' tote bag! And it was right in the middle of Lauren Daigle singing 'Come Alive' on Spirit FM."

The fact of the matter is that without some supernatural gifting, none of us knows whether a train interrupting our commute was scheduled by enemies of God or by Union Pacific employees. Without divine revelation, none of us can prove the power went out because of spiritual beings instead of power grid frailties.

What we do know is that those opposed to God are opposed to his character. They hate who and what he loves. They stand against peace and unity, true love and intimacy, altruism and generosity, humility and mercy. They affront all the elements of God's character. Something or someone wants us to withdraw and hide. Invisible yet dark, a realm of beings wants to drive wedges between friends, family, and cultures. Diabolical powers celebrate death and war. Evil salivates over depression and suicide. Like a 1960s Bond villain, the opposite of heaven roots for chaos. Sinister combatants are clawing at fate, aware of their inevitable demise. Jesus' brother wrote that even the demons believe in the truth of the trinity. So, I'm guessing they've read the book of Revelation.

Whatever is at play in the spiritual stratosphere, I've seen its influence show up at ground level and in street clothes. Its manifestations would rarely alert us to call an exorcist. No, it typically shows up as lies we tell ourselves, fibs we tell others, and deception we absorb from culture. Darkness shows up with a sleight of hand trick. Malevolence misdirects our attention. It makes us think the enemy is our spouse, our boss, or someone with a different holy book.

The oft-blamed spiritual warfare very well might have something to do with how many red traffic lights we encounter on the way to church or counseling. But I can't prove you wrong any more than you can prove you're right. What I've found is that spiritual warfare happens less obviously in my surroundings and more blatantly in my thoughts—especially the kind that feel tangible in my chest.

When affected by the invisible forces that the Apostle Paul described, I question others' motives. The accuser makes me question my own too. Bitterness festers. So does mistrust. My autonomy feels threatened and goes into protection mode. Competition rises, and little aspects of life become zero-sum games. The lenses through which I see the world divide everything between mine and not mine. Those glasses might as well be the kind we wear to look at the sun during an eclipse because I'm filtering the world through darkness.

I know I'm not alone in this because our governments have situation rooms. Hundreds of thousands of refugees congregate at national borders and huddle in resettlement camps. Tens of millions more are displaced and dream of making it to those squalid conditions. More than 400,000 people on our planet each year die by homicide. Almost 1,000 people a week commit suicide in "the land of the free and the home of the brave." According to the Centers for Disease Control, a couple in the United States gets divorced every 40 seconds. Twitter and Facebook fights happen even more often than that. If you doubt the inherent depravity of humanity, please check out the comment section of any significantly played video on YouTube.

It's not just anonymous stats. We've all heard someone say a racial slur. We've all heard someone use inappropriate labels for people with different sexual ethics from our own. We've all scrolled past memes posted by friends or family, comparing political opponents to animals, to Hitler, to human waste, or to those with mental disabilities. I can't speak for how this has seeped into your church experience. But as a kid, I remember a church business meeting with yelling and pointing—and then Sunday services with half the attendees.

It's not just other people. We are all broken. We've all aimed our ire at a friend's tent instead of the bear on top of it. We've all given ourselves the benefit of the doubt but withheld it from others. We've all skipped a day or four hundred in praying for our enemies. We're all scoring points for the wrong team. We're all accomplishing goals Jesus didn't list.

That's why I have to remind myself often: "Shoot high. That could just as well be me on the bottom." I have to remember that I have more in common with others than I'd like to admit. I have to remind myself I'm looking at someone who also bears the image of God. I have to admit that most people aren't bears; they just sleep in different tents. I have to remember we're all hearing whispers from forces of hate and anarchy. I have to aim my attention higher. Sometimes, that means praying for the combatant. Sometimes, that means serving the irritant. Sometimes, it's just simply acquiescing and praying the centering prayer I learned from John Eldredge, "Lord, I give everyone and everything to you." Between you and me, I regularly have to slowly repeat that prayer a few times out loud to lower my heart rate and raise my aim.

How prayer works is still a mystery, even to the greatest theologians. Somehow, our ignorance assimilates with God's omniscience. In a seemingly random algorithm, our myopia impacts his pervasive experience. In asymmetric patterns, our tunnel vision influences his sovereignty. None of us know how to change God's mind. Nobody can predict when we might change his plan. Even the richest human can't hire data scientists to help anyone game the system, if there even is a system. All of us can, however, allow our prayers to change us. We can surrender our wants and wills. Each of us can follow that relinquishing with behavior that proves it. We can extend mercy and grace, patience and kindness. We can leverage humility to pray for blessings to fall on campers in other tents and even people we mistake as bears.

We'll never give Jesus intel he doesn't already know. We don't have to worry that he might mistake us for bears. Thankfully, none of us have to tell Jesus where to aim his justice. His eternal consequences are already established. Those truths help me sleep better—even on subfreezing nights when I smell like carbs in bear country.

A STORM TO THE RESCUE

An unconventional path to our destiny.

I like canoeing and camping. I had never combined the two pastimes until a journey down the Big Otter River. The Big Otter starts where Sheep Creek and Little Stony Creek meet at the base of Sharp Top Mountain. It then zigzags around farms, granite cliffs, and even a bamboo forest before it dumps into a bigger river that takes its water all the way to the Atlantic Ocean.

A baker's half dozen of us cut out of work early on a summer Friday afternoon to paddle from our buddy's house to a farm about halfway to the dirt parking lot where our vehicles were parked. HB, who led our expedition, had gotten permission from the farmer's wife for us to camp on their property. As dusk stole the sun, we paddled up to the farm. The farmer had been standing between the trees on the left side of the river, waiting for us. When we got up close to the bank, he told us to scoot along down the river. He didn't want the insurance risk of strangers on his property.

This was bad news. We now had canoes with tents, an ice chest of breakfast food, and a stove—but no place to set up and significantly less than an hour of daylight left. We were coming up on a highway bridge and a big choice. We could call off the second day of the trip with a phone call to one of our wives. We could ask her to retrieve a pair of shuttle drivers and take them to the takeout. Or we could slide into the shadows and hope to find a secluded place to set up emergency shelter.

We chose the latter option. We also chose not to use headlamps so that our eyes would adjust to less and less light. If my memory serves me right, we withdrew from conversation after a bit to listen to the water. We didn't have to be quiet to hear a distant rumble, though. And then another. The unevenness of the sound let us know the source wasn't big rigs on the highway bridge back upstream.

That was thunder.

Thunder meant lightning, and lightning meant we had to find shelter as quickly as possible. Andrew took off along the bank, scouting options while the rest of us slid down the relative safety of the center of the inky, black current.

The banks were steep here. I couldn't see lights from any houses. Andrew shouted for us on river right. He had found a tiny stream into which we could paddle to get out of the river's push. Now, the thunderclaps came after a strobe-lit sky revealed details of our surroundings. I did that thing where you count how many seconds between the flash and the bang. We didn't have much time. What had been a calm-weather float was about to get hairy.

As we took turns clawing our way up the slippery banks, we could hear both wind and rain pelt leaves in the distance. So as not to draw attention from the landowner, we didn't use our lights as we scurried to tie off the canoes and erect our tents in a stranger's backyard. HB heard dogs barking from up by the house. Now the rain was slapping the leaves around us, and the lightning was bright enough to see each other's faces. We ducked into our respective tents to get out of the rain.

I wiggled into my sleeping bag in Aaron's tent. The deafening crackle of thunder made Hollywood B movie sound effects jealous. Lightning seemed to strike as close as the other side of the river— maybe closer. As rain tapped and then hammered on our tent, our world went from black to bright and immediately back to black. I don't think I've ever been so scared in a tent in my life.

A half hour or so later, the storm had passed. Then I passed out for the night.

We woke early to a bustling river. The torrent had dumped clay and construction silt into the river, which churned with sediment until it looked like chocolate milk. We tore down camp in minutes. No fire. Fathers explained to their sons in low voices that we needed to be silent. We slid down the banks into our boats and then slipped down the stream back into the Big Otter.

With rumbling stomachs we started looking for some shoals or unkept land where we could pull over for breakfast. Right off the bat, though, we came upon a rock ledge that spanned all but maybe 15 percent of the river's width. In the daytime, it took some maneuvering to avoid its danger using a small channel on the river's far left side. The night prior, we had been out in the middle while Andrew scouted on the right. In utter darkness, we all would most likely have dumped. If the thunder and lightning hadn't forced us to find immediate refuge, our night float could've included us losing gear and maybe even canoes while we tried to swim in a rising, black river.

This sounds weird, but Jesus sent a storm to rescue us.

I don't know how that sentence sits with you. Maybe you just see this experience as a coincidence or dumb luck. Maybe your faith doesn't allow for God to add a blessing to our poor decisions. Maybe you don't have a category for a God who would leverage a scary thing to do his work. Maybe your clock winder just lets consequences run their course with little or no interruptions.

I think we all can agree, though, that benevolent coincidences happen all the time. We've all seen the stories on Facebook or the nightly TV news. Someone was in the right place at just the right time, and now at least two lives are inexorably changed. We could have a good debate about sovereignty and luck, faith and chance. But that's not why I tell this story—and not just because we can't use empirical evidence to prove either side of that debate.

No, I tell that story for those open to the metaphysical with a different question. Do you think Sovereignty can use unconventional means to pursue our hearts?

I do.

I'm not here to discount your life experience, but I can tell you multiple stories of Jesus leveraging pain, loss, tragedy, and even hard consequences to demonstrate his love and bring life. My buddies have lost their marriages but found their Rescuer. My friends have lost their children but gained an indescribable closeness with their Father. I've watched financial hardship bring an endearing dependence on The Provider whose balance sheet doesn't use numerals. Great trauma has turned into great empathy. Death has led to new life. Obstacles have stopped atrophy and developed faith muscles.

I've endured storms in my life that pushed me across a river of my own dysfunction. I've heard the thunder in friends' lives, as Sovereignty benevolently changed the trajectory of their journeys. I've watched lightning flash and then reveal a loving community, a sense of camaraderie, and then beautiful unity. We've been pelted with precipitation, as the Rainmaker washes away our brokenness.

Even though storms surprise us, Jesus isn't surprised by anything in our lives. He doesn't run a parallel universe deal where he plays out all of the scenarios somewhere else.

He's just sovereign.

Jesus is not constrained by our choices, our forecasts, or our religious assumptions. He doesn't need to follow our guidelines or timelines, our preferences or expectations. He doesn't have to play by our rules. Personally, I'm glad that God doesn't do things my way because I make a poor god. That last sentence has cost me six figures' worth of real money. It has cost me hours of sleep and tablespoons of tears. Trying to be my own god, I've not seen God on his way to me. I've not recognized that he was working a rescue. I've not always appreciated that reality in the moment, but I've learned to trust his heart.

More than ever before, I like to know when lightning is coming my way. I now have the Lightning app on my phone. It alerts me when bolts strike within twenty-five miles of my current location. It's one of only a few apps on my phone from which I allow notifications. I can't tell you how many times I have felt my phone buzz, looked out my window, and seen blue skies. I read in an article about wilderness safety that lightning can strike thirty miles from clouds under a clear blue sky. Maybe that's where we got the phrase *out of the blue*. What may look like someone else's storm might actually impact our journey. This has happened in my faith journey multiple times—when someone else's cancer or job loss or unfaithful spouse has required growth in me to walk with them. At other times, the surprise was never anyone else's but mine.

I'm grateful, though, that Jesus has never used a storm to ruin me. The Gardner has used lightning to tear into the soil of my façades. The Voice of Many Waters has used thunder to help me realize my unsafe reality and habits. The God of Thunder has let rumbles permeate my heart like a sonogram, revealing fears and insecurities. Omnipotence has redirected rain-swollen rivers to wash and reveal the roots of my improper motives, my disingenuous acts of service. He has let hurricanes and tornadoes tear off the roof of my life so that he could rebuild something much better.

Whether or not you or I like it, he sends storms to the rescue. Maybe because nobody else would. And maybe because that's what it takes to get us to leave where we are and rejoin him on the adventure that he destined for us.

WIDGEON LAKE

When yes means I love you.

My favorite stretch of concrete in the world lines Coal Harbour. Yes, that's the proper spelling; you'll find it on a map of British Columbia. It's a tiny inlet off Vancouver's shipping corridor. Opposite of this stretch of sidewalk, the Stanley Park peninsula protects the shallow water from the wakes of tankers and cargo ships. A row of snowcapped Canadian Rockies loom over the tops of the trees that contrast scores of white sailboat masts. Colorful, little houseboats huddle between multi-million-dollar yachts. Skyscrapers of green or blue glass stand guard. Rowing sculls glide through the mist across the dormant dawn water, their oars touching the surface like mosquito feet. Floatplanes bob next to floating docks a few hundred feet from the park benches where

I like to watch the sunrise, especially on a Sunday morning. It's one of the places that come to mind when I think about the concept of sabbath.

British Columbia calls my name more than any corner of the planet. Vancouver has a whole room to itself in the home of my heart. Almost every time I return there, I bring someone new. I love introducing friends and family to new experiences and especially to places and pastimes I love.

A few summers ago, I brought my mom out to Vancouver for a birthday weekend. We rode electric bicycles around the sea wall, visited exquisite gardens, ate breakfast in an outdoor café, rode a chair lift over grizzly bears, tasted curry for the first time, toured in tiny water taxis, and visited artisan food shops for indelible treats. Mom got to see the Pacific Ocean and sleep more than two time zones from home for the first time. She flew in the largest and smallest planes in which she'd ever taken a seat. We took our first ever selfie together.

I brought her to those Coal Harbour benches to watch the floatplanes take off and land. It was magical. Shoulder to shoulder, we overheard quiet conversations in multiple other languages punctuated by the piercing buzz of De Havilland Otters and Beavers. It was probably the first time in thirty years that I'd spent a Sunday morning with my mom that didn't include a church service, but my soul felt full. I had been praying about this morning. Two of my close friends had also prayed over it with me atop a Blue Ridge Mountain a few days prior. I felt God blessing those prayers as anticipation swelled within me.

I watched my mom's body language, trying to gauge whether she felt excitement or anxiousness. See, in about ninety minutes we were scheduled to board one of those amphibious birds—the smallest one in the fleet, actually. I was stoked. Floatplanes are one of my favorite ways to fly. If I were ever to get my private pilot's license, it would be almost exclusively to fly one.

Mom hid her anxiety well. I didn't tell her that our plane was as old as she was. We found out later that our pilot had never flown this specific tour until that flight. After surrendering the coolest boarding passes you've ever seen, we slid onto the bench seat behind our pilots. It held only a couple of lap belts and looked like it had been pulled out of an old school bus. Not your typical exit row.

We taxied out to the shipping channel, and the pilot gunned the throttle. My smile reached my ears, which were full of a guttural noise that'd make a Harley Davidson jealous. Our takeoff barely cleared the road deck of the Lions Gate Bridge, a Kelly green version of San Francisco's Golden Gate Bridge. I wouldn't be surprised if our Beaver's floats sprinkled harbor water onto a couple of the cars on the road deck below. As the channel widened into the ocean, we banked right and headed up along the mountains that slope into Howe Sound.

A few minutes later, we banked again to head into rugged, untamable mountains. We skirted spires and snaked around peaks. I'd never flown so close to rocks in an airplane. Our little plane bounced through alpine thermals and over plunging slopes. If you had told me we were living in a National Geographic documentary, I wouldn't have questioned you. I took turns looking at the unreal vistas outside of my window and watching my mom do the same—her iPhone perched at her shoulders, waiting for the next capture.

After almost an hour, we flew over a gorgeous alpine lake. Our captain looked steeply down through his door's window. Then the co-pilot motioned the approach pattern. I snagged Mom's attention, emphatically pointed down, and mouthed "We're going down!" She told me later that my eyes were huge. I pumped my fist rapidly. Our wings dipped a touch to the right to widen our pattern and then hard to the left. We twisted down until we were flying straight at a gorgeous waterfall that spilled out of the lake between towering conifers. I watched the falls disappear under the pontoon beneath my window. Seconds later, I watched that pontoon slide onto a midnight-blue lake. The pilot slid our plane into the middle of the lake, and then the old Beaver shook as the propeller sputtered to a stop.

Our pilots exited the aircraft on their respective sides and welcomed us out onto the narrow floating platforms. No life jackets. No safety briefing. Just an invite. The amorous couple from the back bench stepped out with the instructor, and Mom and I joined the rookie pilot on the other side. We took turns, bending down to dip our fingers into the cold, dark water. I took a big inhale of the kind of air that deodorants and laundry detergents falsely promise. The young captain told us the lake had been frozen solid just a month earlier. He then snapped a picture of Mom and me under the wing. It's my favorite picture with her ever.

We returned to our seats after only a few, seemingly stolen minutes. We buckled up as the captain fired up the clamoring pistons. With the mountains to our back and sides, our Beaver thundered toward the trees and then over them. The forest floor instantly fell thousands of feet, and we banked toward Vancouver. Minutes later, we splashed down in front of approving skyscrapers and puttered over to the floating docks. Mom and I slowly walked up the metal ramp to the seawall and then into the gift shop, where she bought me a couple of hats that I wear only on special occasions.

Every time I wear one of those hats, I think about that Sunday morning. And you know what? As epic as the flight and the lake were, my favorite memory of the experience didn't occur inside the plane or on its port-side pontoon. It happened on that sliver of concrete that separates Vancouver from its harbor.

I asked Mom, "Were you scared?"

"Yes," she answered "But I trusted you."

Whether she knew it or not, my mom had never said "I love you" so emphatically to me in her entire life. I wasn't flying the plane, but she trusted me.

She saw my heart for her.

She believed I wasn't trying to traumatize her.

She knew I wanted what was best for her.

She surrendered her fear to that love.

She traded her reality for the unknown, and mystery gave way to knowing.

She experienced an adventure she would never have attempted herself.

As I've thought back multiple times on that trip, I've heard an internal whisper from that voice that isn't a voice, just a knowing from The One Who Knows You. "That's how I feel when you trust me. That affection—that warmth, that full heart—that's what I feel when you surrender to me." I'm not trying to put words in God's mouth. I just felt a new and unique kinship with him because of this episode. It's like one of those country songs when a son finally realizes what a dad told him at his wedding was true.

I can also relate to my mom in this encounter, though. She confided that she was glad she experienced it but that once was enough. I totally get that, and I wouldn't push her to go again. Spiritually, I've been where she was physically: when that last surrender is enough. I'm good for a while. I'm glad I did it. I don't regret it, anyway. But I'd like to keep what's left of my control and comfort for a bit longer.

I'd like to protect more of my freedom, more of my money, more of my autonomy. I'd like to hold onto more of my naps, more of my Saturday mornings, more of those Facebook likes. Too often, I prefer to keep my impure words, my bitterness, and my collection of praise.

I'm not ready to step onto a bobbing floatplane of secret serving. I'm not ready to climb up onto a bench of forgiveness. I don't want to untie from the dock of habits, piety, and recognition.

We all have docks to which our surrender is tied. Your secure docks are probably just as understandable from a therapist's perspective as mine are, and they're probably just as safe. They might even be scenic—home to beautiful comfort. We can be grateful for our comfort and thank Jesus for it, but comfort is rarely the soil in which we grow the most. I probably shouldn't speak for you. From my experience, though, my relationship with Jesus gets more intimate and fruitful when I'm hurting, weary, or unsure. He hears from me more often when there's turbulence on my flight, when my plane is loud and doesn't have wheels, when I'm jealous of my pilot's five-point harness from my lap-belt seat. I feel Sovereignty's presence when I have to trust his heart in spite of what I see out the window.

I know this, but I still resist the stretching. My sunglasses filter Heaven's invitations as trials, even though I know he has a better view and a better plan than I do. The truth that God knows better is in my hard drive somewhere—just not on my desktop. I'm really good at referencing it and quoting it to others—just not to my own heart. When I do apply it to my story, it's often not until the epilogue. Maybe that's why God keeps bringing new faith challenges my way: to improve my memory or to give me more mnemonic triggers.

Maybe, then, it's no coincidence that C.S. Lewis had a beaver declare his famous line about Aslan, the Christ figure: "Who said anything about safe? 'Course he isn't safe. But he's good. He's the King, I tell you." It was in a Beaver floatplane where I watched that good, unsafe King's heart on display. I now have a Facebook album, some Instagram photos, and a couple of sick hats—all with a De

Havilland Beaver on them—to remind me to trust his heart. Those join many other altars from other adventures that he probably hopes will spur my surrender in the years ahead.

So much of my faith walk used to be making sure I was standing on the right dock to wait for the flight to heaven. You know: believe the right stuff; maintain attendance and tithing; avoid the big no-no's. I heard from pulpits that Jesus saved special rewards for missionaries and martyrs, but they seemed like another caste, an unattainable example. For sure, I still hope they get something special throughout eternity for their epic choices and unfathomable sacrifices. That said, I've since learned that Jesus called *all* of us to follow him—to keep moving in such a way that proves we believe him, that we trust his heart. He teaches while he walks—or in this analogy, while he flies. His voice can only be heard if we keep moving too—if we get on the floatplane.

The spiritual life is a journey through his kingdom, and our growth won't get very far if we never leave the dock. We've got tickets waiting for lots of tours with Jesus and dozens of sorties for him. He's saved us seats on flights across the street, across town, and across arbitrary boundaries that we've drawn to hedge our comfort. He wants me to trust his heart. He wants you to trust his love.

He waits on that pontoon with excitement, knowing we'll thank him later. He waits in the front seat with anticipation, knowing our reviews will sound a lot like, "I love you."

THE PILLOW PIT

Home is where you surrender.

I'm writing this chapter from my pillow pit.

"A pillow what?" you might ask.

Several years ago, I bought a bunch of run-of-the-mill bed pillows and even more fabric. My kid sister and I secretly sewed pillowcases for enough pillows to fill the bed of my buddy Scotty's pickup. On the afternoon of my wedding anniversary, I covered the pillows with blankets and secured them with a cargo net. Then, I drove my wife and some picnic food up to a scenic overlook on the Blue Ridge Parkway. We ate dinner, watched the sunset, and welcomed the moonrise from under our autumn blankets. It was a beautiful evening made magical by millions of stars.

The next day, I carried all the pillows up to my office before returning Scotty's F-150. I now had a bigger stash of pillows than populates a Victorian bed and breakfast. So, I framed a box out of eight-foot-long sheets of corrugated metal roofing. I threw the pillows in the above-ground pit only to learn how much bigger it was than a pickup bed. My stash of pillows looked more like a pile of laundry than a fluffy ball pit. I'm not joking: it takes the cargo area of 1.3 Suburbans with all rear seats folded down to equal the cubic feet of my office pillow pit.

Over the years since I built the pillow pit, I've pursued a series of small goals for my business. As I achieved each mile marker, I bought another pillow. I recently changed the reward system, because the box is now brimming with more than a hundred pillows, cushions, and bean bags on top of an old queen-size mattress.

My nieces and nephews love climbing up onto the padded frame and then jumping into the cloud of pillows. Or doing a trust fall into them. I do too. We play peekaboo and hide 'n' seek under the pillows. We tickle each other while fully immersed in pillows that differ in shape, density, and surface texture. Some have embroidered art. Some feel like a shaggy pet. Some are slick but squishy like a chunky baby right after a bath in the kitchen sink. Together, they feel like a hug when you're burrowed under them. Some nights, I sleep under them—creating the thickest weighted blanket you've ever seen.

I've worked from home for almost two decades. I get cabin fever all the time. Okay, everyday. Actually, several times a day. When I can't flee to another country or an American wilderness, I escape to my pillow pit. It's a calming place for me—like the hugging machine that the autistic inventor, Temple Grandin, built for herself. That quicksand of fluffiness embodies comfort. That mountain of pillows invites rest. It represents a lot of what many of us attribute to the word *home*. Only people close to my heart have been in it.

Rest is an underrated component of adventure. I've learned firsthand that premeditated rest makes any adventure more enjoyable. It makes adrenaline rushes less disorienting. It improves my ability to process adventures afterwards too. Our bodies weren't designed to run long-term on adrenaline. Our senses have limits and alarm systems for overload. We come wired from the factory with shutdown protocol. We don't just need sleep. Our bodies crave rest. Our souls long for comfort. Our psyches are like GPS units: constantly recalculating when we stray from the easiest path. Our hearts need some semblance of normalcy.

Over time, I've realized that rest is more than sleep or even inactivity and that it's okay to find that catharsis in different ways than other people do. For me, rest can be writing in my journal or taking a shower long enough to test the water heater. Rest can be crying after a movie or riding a bike through a foreign city. Its soundtrack can be meaningful music, comical podcasts, or authentic audiobooks. My mind switches to airplane mode while driving fast on winding, country roads or sitting atop a hill, watching the sunset.

When responsibilities and limitations get overwhelming, I drive up to a dirt patch on the shaded side of North Fork Road. It's guarded across the road by a tiny church building from the 1830s that opens for services once a month. In a camp chair or on a sleeping bag, I plop next to the North Fork of the Tye River, soaking in its sounds and smells and cooler temperature outside of cell service. Whether spring-fed water trickles by or a storm pumps whitewater between its shady banks, I can physically feel my fuel tank gurgling fuller.

As tranquil as this spot is, I struggle to sit in a moment long enough to refill past a quarter of a tank on the gauge. *That's enough gas to get me to my next stopping point*, I think while fidgeting. I don't have an attention span for rest. Rest isn't easy for me. Ironically, it's often work. And sometimes—you can ask my doctor—rest physically hurts because it's such a hard right turn from the pace and pressure of my life. My muscles angrily protest their way to relaxation. Even in my pillow pit.

Despite this, rest has become profoundly more impactful for me. Even when physically exhausted, I've felt the floater on my soul gauge clinking against the top of its tank. Adrenaline rushes still reliably purge stress from my body. Climbing mountains or paddling rivers still helps me collapse into deep sleep. Those don't happen in any reliable rhythm in my life, though. Busyness and business steer me away from the places and pastimes that flesh out words like *rest* and *sabbath*. In all of that noise, despite the frenetic blur, I have been actively fighting for rest in my body and soul.

I get to that place in a counterintuitive way. I surrender.

Jesus promised rest for our souls. He called the weary and those with burdens to his rest. In the middle of that promise, he explained how: we have to follow him and pull with him in his farm yoke. We have to stop when he does, like he does. We also have to keep up with him, slow down with him, and work with him. This alternating sequence isn't always physically relaxing. Ask the guys who traveled with him a couple of millennia ago. It's work. But he rewards that commitment with a presence and pleasure that fill your chest cavity with something other than just deep yoga breaths.

As I've sacrificed my time, energy, and money for Jesus, he's given me scenic overlooks filled with jumping euphoria and tear-soaked healing. As I've granted Jesus access to more of my life, he's occupied that space. Just a heads up, though: surrender is expensive. That relinquishing often demands physical, relational, and financial sacrifices. I've had to let go of dreams. I've wrestled so hard with releasing my grip that the hands of my soul cramped. Between you and me, those moments or seasons often suck. But the reward?

Oh, man.

When you see what God was up to, it gives you a sense that you're in the right place at the right time. When Jesus' influence on you eventuates in a positive life change in someone else, you feel part of the supernatural. When you experience vulnerable, authentic moments with other Jesus followers, you connect with something bigger than yourself. When a miracle happens or something broken is restored, your soul says, "Yes! This is good!" You feel compelled to tell everybody ALL THE THINGS, and you need more exclamation marks. You feel full. More than full, you feel hot goodness spilling out of the mug of your life.

In those moments, your looming bills don't matter. During those encounters, demands and deadlines at work stand in the blurry edges of your peripheral vision, if visible at all. In those seasons, your obstacles seem surmountable. You feel fueled for challenges, refueled for your assignments. The nozzle on your gas pump jerks. The trigger clicks off. Your tank is full: full of gratitude, full of wonder, full of worship.

That's rest. That's sabbath. That's home.

Home has changed for me over the years, as I've gone on both physical and spiritual adventures. Part of Jesus' continual Advent is realized in a weird kind of rest, a different sense of comfort, a new reason for home. Comfort for the sake of comfort can lead us to atrophy. It can cause us to withdraw from growth. Home has become the restorative base from which I launch into the uncomfortable. Not an address, not a mattress, not even a pillow pit, home is the place where I plug my heart into its USB cord. Home is wherever Jesus refuels me for the next surrender, the next assignment. That connective recharging has happened next to glaciers and icebergs, on mountains and rivers. But Jesus has also refueled me in garages and basements, in driveways and parking lots, at picnic tables and fire pits.

You and I have different red lines on our life tachometers. Our fuel tanks come in different shapes and sizes too. What fills our love locker, our serotonin levels, and the wells of our souls varies wildly. But all of us can find an uncanny rest in obedience. When we pursue surrender more than comfort, we find a reward that permeates our cells and our psyche. When we relinquish ourselves to Jesus, we find rest for our souls.

No amount of pillows on the planet can compete with that.

INDUCTION DAY

Failure is a feature—not a bug—of spiritual adventure.

I wish you knew my friend, Tanner. You'd brag about him too. I was born during the Carter administration. Tanner joined the planet around the same time we got Napster and Myspace, but he has insight beyond his years. My jaw has literally dropped during the years of our friendship, hearing about what he has accomplished.

Here's how I described it to our Senator and House Representative in the letters of recommendation I wrote several years ago:

> *I'm writing to recommend your consideration of Tanner*
> *for nomination to the United States Naval Academy. He*
> *is a leader of men, an example of the best of America's*

next generation.

I have served with him on our church's parking team for the past several years. We are a team of more than forty that serve a church body of more than 3,500 weekly attendees. Though considerably younger than the majority of his teammates, he has been an area leader and trainer for years. In our lots and with our parishioners, he displays the same commitment to excellence that he has leveraged for sports and academics.

Rarely have I seen someone with the ambitious drive or the relational awareness of this young man—let alone both. Having spent half of my childhood near Annapolis and having interacted with Naval Academy graduates, I am confident he will lead within that great institution as he has led here.

Fast forward to the sweltering heat today in Annapolis, where the superintendent of the United States Naval Academy addressed Tanner and 1,213 other midshipmen. In his induction speech, the commanding officer acknowledged that the men and women before him were America's elite high school graduates. He told them of the 13,000 who had applied to the service academy that year but had not been accepted. (He had told the plebes' parents earlier in their briefing that this incoming class owned the highest average SAT and ACT scores of any previous incoming class.)

"Some of you have never failed at anything," the man in dress whites declared. "Over the next few days and weeks, you will fail. We plan for you to fail. We will push you to your limit. We want to see you learn how to get back up, how to rely on each other to succeed."

I don't know if the teenagers in front of me absorbed that line, but it pierced me like an arrow. I'm not an elite student nor any kind of athlete. I've never surrendered my life in the country's service, either. I have, though, enjoyed success in most of my pursuits in life. And I do mean enjoy. Not that life's been easy, but it has been incredibly rewarding. Only a few dreams I've chased didn't happen.

Until last summer.

I got fired for the first time at thirty-nine years old. More accurately, I was not offered a contract renewal. I had been teaching continuing education—something I absolutely loved—around the country on behalf of two sister organizations for about half a decade. I had taught in hotel and convention centers through their parent nonprofit for a dozen years. Those seminar trips kept me out of the office four or five weeks a year, but I got a *lot* of affirmation out of the deal. Attendees raved about my presentations in person and in the course evaluations. A few of them even became clients.

I didn't take the un-hiring well. Suspicion shadowed my friendships. I questioned my content and even my own character. Like a dumped high school romance, I bounced from insecurity to insolence. I oscillated between trying to prove myself valuable in other areas to declaring, "I don't need them!" I quit teaching for the sister organization and withdrew from the parent nonprofit's other events.

I could see the adventure inherent in the Plebe Summer waiting for Tanner—the challenges and maybe even his potential failures. His superintendent made me realize, though, that I hadn't seen my own stress tests and failures as part of my future success. I certainly hadn't viewed it as a device to make the plot in the story of my life more interesting. I hadn't until then connected it to the challenge that comes with every grand adventure. I didn't sit down in that failure and absorb it. I was too busy trying to spin it, redeem it, or use it as fuel for the next thing—whatever that would be.

What I needed to do was ponder what God might want to accomplish with the new vacancy in my life. Jesus doesn't have room to bring his newness into a life filled with our old stuff. We might not see our comfort or habits or accomplishments as old. We definitely don't see them as expendable. We tend not to realize that a part of us is replaceable until it's forcefully removed. Jesus often needs to excavate a place to make room for his Immanuel-ness, his Advent.

He regularly prunes even good things—unfailures—to make new growth possible.

My contract not being renewed became the catalyst for Jesus to do new things in my life. With no speaking commitments, I gained time for exploring new places instead of well-worn hotel conference rooms. I've been more available for mentoring conversations that come with a lot of affirmation despite no speaker evaluations. I got extra time to do billable work and to write this book. I realized my friends didn't love me any less and that I was no less valuable to the world.

It took a military ceremony for me to realize my failure was a feature, not a bug, of my spiritual adventure. I now have something in common with Bible legends. Noah got naked drunk. Moses killed a critic. Samson let a seductress cut his hair. David killed the husband of his rape victim. Solomon forsook his wisdom. Peter had to be told, "Get behind me, Satan." I had let embarrassment become bitterness.

Jesus isn't intimidated by our failures. We don't jeopardize the ending of his story with our mistakes or even our sins. He's bigger than our denouncements, our defections, and our heresy. He mourns for the pain we bring on ourselves and on others, but he knew our maturity would require chances to use our independence the wrong way.

This was pictured for me last week. My sister posted a photo of my toddler nephew after he dressed himself. In the picture, Bear modeled a Patagonia trucker hat, a tractor T-shirt, tiny shorts, and fancy dress shoes. He picked everything out, and he beamed with pride. He's been working for weeks to put on his own shoes and then to get them on the right feet. The little dude walked out into the world and its sunshine with mismatched clothes. My sister didn't scold him, didn't frown at his odd choices, didn't tell him he could've done better. Emily knew Bear had just moved one step closer to the fully formed person he'll be one day.

Jesus lets me leave the house many days looking like my nephew. Sometimes, I pull the right clothes out of the closet but with the wrong motives. Other times, I assemble outfits that make no sense. Jesus lets the world see my sweet behavioral shoes that don't match my bitterness shirt. He lets me flaunt both my theologically profound hat and my glutinous pants. It's not that Heaven likes the outfit or that he wants me to look like that. He just knows I'm on a journey. I will always be somewhere on the left side of the continuum of my full potential.

Jesus isn't embarrassed by my failure. He doesn't cheer for it, either. He doesn't celebrate my immaturity, nor does he plan to leave me where I left the path. I'll let theologians debate whether he brings failure to us or just the freedom to find it ourselves. What I do know is that I'm no less his child when I screw up. He doesn't see me through the lens of those sins, those mistakes, those momentum killers.

If you're like me, you've got a bunch of scabs on your spiritual knees and elbows. Maybe even your chin. You've let go of kindness balloons that flew away. You've accidentally shredded official forms of grace. You've driven a car into the anger ditch. Okay, maybe it was a tractor trailer. Maybe it's real world failures. You've flunked out of school, declared bankruptcy, or broke your wedding vows. The consequences bring waves of pain. The regret reverberates until your ears ring. Everything hurts.

If so, you're in the right spot. Maybe not the best spot, but you're standing on dirt in which Jesus can grow something new. That's what he does. You've walked a few steps into an adventure, even if you don't know what adventure it is yet. The important thing to know is that Jesus does. He knows where you're headed, what he can grow in that soil, what could bloom into something beautiful. Sovereignty is not surprised. The Prince of Peace is not frantic. Omnipotence is not thwarted.

This isn't his first Plebe Summer—not even close. He's still here to walk with us through our toddlerhood, our grade school years, and that awkward middle school season. He's rooting for you and me to learn how to match our shirts and pants before we get to those high school yearbook pictures.

HOLE IN THE ROOF

Rudolph, why's your smile so bright?

In January of 2014, while my wife was out of the country on a missions trip, I headed over to Cape Town to pre-write several months' worth of commercial blog posts. There's no short way to South Africa from the States, even when leaving from the East Coast. Like everyone else behind the curtain on the plane, I arrived tired and determined to collapse into at least half a day of sleep. That intention melted during the taxi ride to my hostel in Green Point. My curiosity to absorb the neighborhood overtook my exhaustion.

I set out on foot toward the stadium where Nelson Mandela's funeral had been held just a month earlier. Despite all the Googling that preceded the trip, I had failed to realize that the African Nationals

Championship was in town. Sixteen futbol teams had converged on Green Point at the same time I had. The rumble of their fans and the hum of vuvuzelas poured out onto the streets. Host nation South Africa was playing as I walked past the silver basket of a stadium. The air was electric, and I forgot to feel tired.

A man walked up to me on the sidewalk and asked if I'd like to buy tickets for the next match. In the States, we'd call the dude a scalper. Maybe he was. But I found the $9 ticket price to be a bargain. (The evening's event was a double header, and most people bought just the early match because of the home team. So, there were thousands of seats available for the second game.) I'd never been to an international match. I had just read Bob Goff's *Love Does* and felt a compulsion to say "Yes!" to new things—despite my jet lag. So, I handed the man some Rands from my pocket and headed down to the waterfront to kill time before the second match would start.

Something inside me whispered, "That's a good start. Now try something bigger." Over the course of the next hour, I walked down to the ocean, found a sandwich shop for dinner, and then headed back toward the stadium. I noticed a small crane—maybe forty or fifty feet tall—leaning out over the harbor and flipped through excuses I could leverage to climb it. I stopped by the security guard shack at one of the docks and asked if I could talk to the loading crane operator. I figured the worst he could say was, "No." And "No," was what I got along with something mumbled about authorized personnel.

The following day, I would feel grateful for that rejection, because Jesus had reserved a bigger adventure. I've lived through a lot of moments like that: where Jesus out-dreams me and when he directs a no to lead to a better yes. So many of my current realities were built on the foundation of prayers that seemed to go unanswered, dreams that weren't big enough, and thoughts not as high as his.

One of those moments happened halfway between those docks and Cape Town Stadium, where a much taller crane loomed from behind a construction fence. I circumnavigated the fence until I got to its entrance. There, I asked the guard if I could interview the crane operator the next morning. He told me to return at 7 o'clock the next morning, and he'd ask the site foreman for me. I hoped the long night shift wouldn't change his mind. I kept looking back at the crane, as I hiked back over to the stadium. Since I had just read his book about serendipitous adventures, I took a picture on my phone and tweeted it to Bob, hoping that'd bring good luck. You know: like touching the hem of his digital garment or something.

I watched Nigeria double up Mozambique in a stadium with 46,000 empty seats. After the first 20 minutes, I slinked down to the front row by the corner kick flag. While colorful and entertaining, the competition and its spectators couldn't fully distract me from the potential adventure of the next morning. The pageantry and noise and movement should've held my attention on the field, but my mind drifted to a crane I couldn't see at the moment. Distracted by the story I hadn't lived yet but couldn't wait to tell, I struggled to enjoy a game my friends back home would've loved to watch in person. I looked up into the stadium's rafters and thought about climbing up there too.

Instead of sleeping in on the following morning, I sprang early to assemble props to make me look official and hiked down to the construction site. I got there way earlier than he had suggested. The gatekeeper was still jolly and had a good memory. He showed me where to go to meet the site foreman, who greeted me with a puzzled face. I explained that I would like to interview his crane operator for my blog. I had no idea how I would turn climbing a crane into a post about advertising. I didn't have a thesis to test. I just tried to make the fake excuse credible. I showed him my laptop, which was wrapped in my company's advertising. I handed him my metal business card, over which he mulled for many, long seconds. I showed him I had brought my own safety helmet (my kayaking helmet with a pair of GoPro mounts on it). He pondered and then obliged, tossing me a neon safety vest. He walked me out to the yard and called out to the crane operator who was walking toward his post.

"Rudolph! This man is going with you."

Rudolph looked puzzled that someone would accompany him. I certainly didn't look like a safety inspector. At the base of his 57-meter tower crane, he asked, "Are you afraid of heights?"

"Not today," I replied.

I don't know how it works in other cranes, but there was no elevator up the tower of this crane. We climbed a series of ladders that switched directions every section so that falling wouldn't drop you the full way to the concrete base. It reminded me of this thing we used to do in our ten-story college dorm. We'd climb the entire fire escape as quickly as possible—but using only the hand railings.

At the top of the last ladder was a metal hatch in the ceiling. Rudolph pushed it up and open, then invited me up into his cab. He closed the hatch behind us, and I stood behind him as he demonstrated the various controls at his disposal. Rudolph beamed with pride, as a stranger from America seemed impressed with what would otherwise be quiet, unassuming work. Then, Rudolph hopped out of his seat and climbed some metal rungs on the wall behind me. He lifted open a roof hatch. Sunlight poured in from the hole in the roof as he invited me out onto the short, weighted arm that counterbalances the crane's jib (the long part from which the hook hangs).

I interviewed Rudolph up there for probably twenty minutes, as we watched the sun rise and warm Table Mountain and Lions Head in the distance. I learned that he would stay up at his post until winds hit north of sixty kilometers per hour. He told me he could lift one and a half or maybe even two tonnes of material at the end of the boom but three tonnes close to his tower base.

To Rudolph, that difference was a matter of fact, a reality of physics. But that disparity hit me like a bucket load of life principle. I had spent the first decade in business trying a lot of work that hung way out at the end of my jib. I had dropped important loads because of it. I had challenged my pulleys and frayed relationship cables. I had tried to prove I could lift stuff fifty feet away from my core competencies.

With that object lesson front and center in my mind, I came home from South Africa with a purpose and plan for simplification that has helped my freelance gig become more effective in fewer things and more profitable overall. Turning away loads at the end of my jib has allowed me to do much more heavy lifting.

I've experienced that principle in ministry and observed it in the lives of other kingdom teammates too. There's so much to do in the kingdom—so many needs, so many hurts, so many opportunities to make a difference. Just in my church alone, there are dozens of different serving teams. We even have a prayer and serving community built around keeping a huge *Finding Nemo* tank at the entrance to our kids ministry in tip-top shape. If you attend any faith-based conferences or listen to Jesus-influenced podcasts, you know there are more organizations doing work for Jesus than there are Starbucks locations. On top of the menu of options, we battle the variety of roles: singing or speaking, blogging or podcasting, fundraising or marketing, teaching or counseling, mentoring or fostering, writing books or creating study guides, photographing or crafting videos, giving medical care or distributing relief supplies, building hospitals or digging wells.

Jesus very much wants to stretch us and make us more reliant on him, and the pursuit of impact and justice in all of those broken realms and ministry environments was his heartbeat before it was ours. But it's easy to get tempted away from our gifting, our calling, and our primary pathways. Some of those roles look more fun, more impactful, and more noteworthy. Parking cars, changing diapers, Cloroxing surfaces, and resetting chairs sometimes doesn't feel big and heavy enough. Keeping that weekly coffee conversation with a coworker going through divorce can seem insignificant. Watching a tired friend's kids so they can have a date night can look less spiritual than a theologian's hours writing a book. The moments and ministries further from our crane's cab can appear more important.

Jesus called his kids to operate different cranes on different job sites. Some of us are called to sit in the cab; others hook up the concrete bucket. Still others pour the concrete. And some of us ride those lawnmower-looking machines that smooth the wet concrete surface. I've never been good with joysticks—definitely not back in the Atari days and not much better on the morning I tried to clear snow in a Bobcat. So, you, Rudolph, and Jesus probably don't want me running a real crane. I really like wearing a reflective vest, though; so, I would probably work best as the ground guy who secures the load on the hook.

That's probably why Jesus assigned me to the parking lots of my church. Tending the incubator that is our parking team is close to my heart, close to my crane's tower. For a lot of the leaders I admire, where I serve would be at the end of their crane's jib—and vice versa. Thankfully, we don't have to run *every*one else's crane or even *any*one else's crane. We don't have to assist on every believer's work site. Our hearts individually and even collectively represent a tiny fraction of the one beating in Jesus' chest. We can express only a fraction of his love, his justice, and his remedy. But that's all he expects from us. That's why he places different burdens in our hearts, different abilities in our bodies, and different people in our paths. He leads us each to those places if we follow him to them.

The less time we spend trying to do someone else's work, the more heavy lifting we can do for the kingdom. The more we leverage our spiritual gifts and inherent personalities, the more productive our work for him will be. The closer we operate to our passion and calling, the more people will want to ask us why we love our jobs.

And the more times we'll get to tell them.

THE RESCUERS

"Get him back in the boat!"

With some notable exceptions, most whitewater rapids are graded on a danger scale of Class I to Class VI with Class V being the most technical you can do in a commercial raft. My brother and I scored the front of the raft for our first whitewater trip that included a Class V rapid. Two other things made that Kaituna River trip notable. First, it pummeled us with warm water from its hot springs source. (Whitewater rivers are typically frigid.) Second, it dropped us over Tutea Falls, the highest commercially navigated waterfall in the world. The force of the drop completely submerged not just our raft but everyone in it. You can't even see our helmets in a pair of the photos from the guide company. All of us paddlers emerged back atop the water gasping and gulping for air.

What a rush! So fun.

Our guide, noting our accents, asked us where we called home in the States. With my brother living seventeen time zones behind her in Maryland and me hailing from Virginia I answered, "Near Washington, D.C." I didn't expect her response.

"What are you doing here? You've got the Gauley River in your backyard!"

She explained that some of the best commercially navigated whitewater in the world wasn't far from my house—that she had traveled there to run it. The convincing Kiwi assigned me to give the Gauley a try. Nine months later, when the Gauley opened for its annual, six-weekend dam release, I obeyed her. Turns out, my buddy, Hutch, had been running it every year for more than a decade. I joined up with him and one of my closest friends, HB, who had guided the Lower Gauley back in the '80s. The Lower Gauley is stout, even though most of the Gauley's reputation comes from the Upper.

We signed up for what's called the "Gauley River Marathon," 26 miles of whitewater in one day with 100 graded rapids, 53 of which rated at Class III or bigger and six of which roared as Class V drops. We told our guide, Jimmy, that we would tip really well if he scared us but not at all if he killed us. I remember Jimmy warning us later that day, "I've not run this line before, but if you guys are game, we can try it." We set an outfitter record that day with 31 rafter ejections. I left the boat involuntarily six times. We completely flipped the raft four times.

After the first four sets of Class V rapids, I commented, "I thought they'd be scarier than that." No joke: a few minutes later, that pride led to me getting stuck in a hydraulic. A hydraulic works like a front-loading washing machine where air is at the top of each vertical spin. I was the laundry in question. At least two guides expertly hit my little trouble spot with throw ropes. I'm talking Aaron Rodgers passes, but I missed both as I kept getting regurgitated. Finally, a guide from another rafting company figured out what was happening and intentionally aimed his raft to hit me. That knocked me down into the river's undercurrent, which spit me out downstream. His customers then yanked me into their boat and dropped me off at Jimmy's raft. My buddy, Will, said I looked white and limp—like a dead body.

Believe it or not, that wasn't my most dangerous ejection of the day. Several hours later, I would be incredibly rescued at the top of our last Class V rapid of the day, a rapid officially labeled on the map as—I kid you not—Pure Screaming Hell. One of the guys Hutch had invited snagged my helmet with a single finger, and then Hutch (a wrestling coach) yanked me to safety while risking his own. To aid the effort, our raft was sideways at the top of the critical plunge. After I landed facedown in the boat, HB, Will, and Jimmy dug two epic paddle strokes and straightened us for a clean drop.

I gained empathy that day for what the whitewater industry affectionately calls "swimmers." In fact, that day, people we encountered at different pullover spots referred to me as *the* swimmer. "Oh, *you're the* swimmer!" Even without two-way radios, the story of my rescue raced miles ahead of our raft.

Whitewater "swimming" isn't always dangerous. There's an international system of guide paddle signals for swimmers to follow. Where to swim and how hard to swim depend on the conditions and the location of all parties involved—what the river gives you. Sometimes, you can float feet-first through a liquid roller coaster until the next calm spot. At other times, you get the shout to find your inner Michael Phelps and freestyle for your life. On occasion, Jimmy points you toward a specific bank or rock—or anywhere but a specific rock. And sometimes he demands concern and urgency from your fellow paddlers with, "GET HIM BACK IN THE BOAT!" (You know it's really bad when he adds, "NOW!") Every so often, trying to rescue a swimmer would endanger the whole boat, and you have to power through some technical sections to a place where the whole squad can pull over and then stage a rescue.

That experience and Jimmy's directives have since become part of my faith community's vocabulary. I remember the first time I heard that language from my parking team mentor, Rick. As he told me about a guy who had strayed from The Way of Jesus, he declared, "We've got to get him back in the boat." Immediately, I knew what he meant. On the river, swimmers almost always float faster than a heavy raft and typically float away from the raft. In a second or two, an ejected paddler can be well out of reach. Our former ministry teammate was in spiritual danger; he could drown from his distance.

It's embarrassing to admit, but I didn't follow Rick's imperative. I didn't chase our drifting teammate other than maybe a text message. I forgot that a rip-roaring trip down the river isn't a success unless we all are in the boat at the end.

I still struggle to remember that.

To be fair, not everybody who leaves the boat wants to be rescued. Sometimes, they swim to shore and look for the nearest trail back up to the road to hitchhike back to the car. When our Guide prompts us to attempt a rescue, though, we need to trust his experience, his knowledge of the river, and his better view from the back of the boat. One of the crazy things about a swimmer extraction is that—aside from a massive weight difference—almost anyone can pull almost any swimmer into the boat. You just hold onto the top of their life jacket and fall back into the boat with them. On the tough ones, you just tag team.

The same holds true in our faith journey. You don't have to be a theologian or a pastor to reach out to a straggler. You don't need to have attended a class to encourage someone, to let them know they belong in the boat, to reach out your paddle for them to stay connected to the raft. When dangerous undercurrents or heavy situations threaten, we can all call in a fellow paddler or two—someone with strength and experience. Listen for the Guide's instructions. In rare circumstances, Jesus gives permission for his followers to keep paddling without rescue for the sake of the raft. (Matthew transcribes this in his account of Jesus' ministry, and Paul writes about it in his letters to new churches.) But that's not a call any one paddler makes alone.

This might sound weird, but you can even rescue someone before they fall out of the boat. On the river, it can be grabbing someone as they're falling out or letting them hold onto your life vest to regain their position. I've witnessed a river veteran pull an incredible sit-up while the paddler behind him held onto his life vest in the middle of a Class V rapid. That CrossFit Games-level power crunch kept a lost paddler in the boat.

I've seen the pre-rescue in real life too. Firsthand. Several years ago, I was burned out in ministry. I loved where I served, but I was running on fumes and frustrations. On one particular Sunday, I was mentally working through an exit strategy—how to walk away. I hadn't discussed this with anyone but my wife. My favorite whitewater addict, HB, has often pulled me out of both literal and spiritual rapids. I don't know if he recognized the struggle or just followed a Sovereign assignment. But on the morning that I almost walked away, I found a torn lid of a box stuffed between my rain boots by the back door at church. That wrinkled cardboard is in my office to this day. The thick Sharpie inscription reads,

Ryan George,
Thanks for
working so hard
on Sunday mornings.
You inspire me &
you inspire others!
Happy to be on your team!
Love ya!
H

That note kept me in the boat. I almost missed seeing Chris come to Christ—and getting to baptize him. I almost missed co-starting a men's spiritual adventure community, whose other two founding members are current neon-vest teammates. I almost missed encounters that have broken my will and shaped my life. I almost missed the reward from mentoring, the empathy of my friends, and the euphoria I feel on my drive home from gatherings with other paddlers. Jesus sent HB to stop the danger at *almost*.

If you're spiritually out of the boat right now, swim back. Grab the T grip of the paddle extended to you. If nobody's reaching, yell to your Guide. Ask him how to survive, what your return should look like.

If you're almost out of the boat, grab onto someone's life vest. Don't worry about paddling right now. Just hang on.

And if you're still in the boat, keep your head on a swivel. While a lot of fellow paddlers fall out when the ride is noisy and frenetic, a good number eject from bumping into unexpected rocks in calm water. When God prompts you to encourage someone, don't hesitate. You don't know what you'll keep from almost happening. And just in case you need to hear this reminder from Paul's letter to his Galatian friends, "Do not grow weary while doing good!"

CLEAN LINES IN THE DIRT

Turns are for fast drivers.

For a short period of time before he moved two time zones away, I enjoyed a friendship with a chef and former street racer named Grinnan. Grinnan raced a modified Subaru WRX and probably acquired flashbacks I don't experience when we're watching *Fast & Furious* movies.

I asked Grinnan one time what was the fastest he'd ever driven. He seemed sheepish about his "165" answer but immediately followed that up with "But I've done 135 sideways."

I thought of Grinnan recently when my racing instructor at DirtFish Rally School explained, "Rally doesn't have corners—just straight and slide." I cheered that line in class, but a little introspection in the months since rally school has made that line convicting. My real life feels like that too—that I have these straight stretches of comfort and accomplishment. And then I'm sliding.

A fractured relationship.

A disheartening discovery.

A nagging physical injury.

A huge, unexpected financial surprise.

A haunting question I can't get out of my head.

A disappointment so huge, it evaporates my gratitude for everything else.

As Jack sketched on the whiteboard in our DirtFish classroom, I wanted so badly to absorb and memorize everything. I knew I wouldn't, though. I struggle with muscle memory on relatively easy processes like shooting a free throw, tossing a corn hole bean bag, or staying in sync with the instructor that one time at my wife's Zumba class. And this wasn't just any kind of driving or even racing. Many experts consider rally the most difficult and dangerous form of auto racing on the planet.

Rally racing requires its drivers to constantly execute counterintuitive maneuvers—like sliding. My whole life, sliding while driving has been a bad situation, a dangerous reality to avoid at all costs. Instead of avoiding the slides, a rally racer and his codriver embrace them. The professionals initiate slides at speeds north of one hundred miles an hour. They know that the faster you go into a slide, the more weight transfers to the downstream wheels which then cut deeper through the dirt and gravel to find the hard-packed ground that offers real traction. That all makes sense in the classroom with illustrations filling digital screens and with diagrams drawn on whiteboards. In a five-point harness behind a mud-splattered windshield, sliding feels uncomfortable to rookies like me—even at much slower speeds.

That's probably why Colin McRae (the youngest person ever to win the World Rally Championship Drivers title) said, "Straight roads are for fast cars. Turns are for fast drivers." By that criteria, I'm not a fast driver—on a rally course or in everyday life. I panic. I pull my foot off the gas too soon. I hit the brakes too hard. I counter-steer too quickly. I lose peripheral vision. That goes for gravel roads and my office, dirt tracks and my kitchen. Back home, the motions are the same. They just look different. I write angry emails. I reach for a credit card. I exclaim words I wouldn't say in front of my mom. My embarrassment, discomfort, and frustration boil into anger that I spew on the wrong people.

Because of the parallels that I was seeing between real life and rally racing, my time at the school illustrated some of my underlying brokenness. It showed me how I've developed wrong defaults on both the track and my spiritual journey. Lessons from a dirt track demonstrated why I've gotten poor results from bad habits and faulty assumptions. DirtFish discoveries reminded me that I often need to unlearn more than I need to learn. Andrew, my in-car instructor, gave me some benefit of the doubt to make me feel better. He attributed a couple of my instincts to my racing experience on asphalt. "That's what you want to do on pavement. It hurts you here on dirt." Despite his generosity, I think we both knew I was just a scaredy-cat on the struggle bus.

It was all just so fast.

Gas.

Break.

Instant 90-degree steering input from hands at 9 and 3.

Wait. Not yet. Wait.

Straighten wheel.

Now gas.

More gas!

This all has to happen in this order. At different parts of the process, several of these steps have to be done in rapid succession. I'm talking in roughly a second. You can't look at gauges or pedals or even the wheel during this sequence. The Subaru is vibrating from the gravel. Your helmet filters the noise unevenly. Your hands breakdance. Thoughts race and then skip, like a YouTube video playing on 3G. It's all a blur. Well, to me, anyway. To the instructor, this was just another day at work. He had enough presence of mind to watch my hands, my feet, and the cones a turn or two ahead on the track. During all of that he inserted directions. His peripheral vision culled and cataloged details my panic missed. He demonstrated this uncanny ability to see the present and the future at the same time. That gave him an admirable patience and a calming presence I've come to expect from another Instructor I know.

I craved commands from Andrew. As the cones got nearer, I wanted to hear his command, "And brake," in my headset. Instead, I backed off the accelerator, which stole momentum for the necessary weight transfer in the slide. Then, I mashed the right pedal before I heard, "Now gas," because I assumed he wanted me to figure out the correct action points on my own on for this lap. Nope. It just wasn't the right time yet. He hadn't overlooked it. Turns out, he knew what he was doing. Crazy, I know. Andrew's conscience-like voice brought beneficial restrictions that led to better slide lines and faster laps.

On the roads of my everyday choices, I'm not so sure I crave that direction. I like navigating my own race, pausing only when I feel unsure or overwhelmed. But on weekdays and weekends, I slide into the proverbial ditch a lot. You'd never think that a towing company would offer some sort of frequent client discount, but I've got one. "Ah,

Mr. George. Carl will be right over. The second curve on 811, again?"

Part of my lack of mature response stems from the same issue I faced in my WRX on the corners at DirtFish, and I mean "faced" literally. A rally driver is supposed to perform all the steps listed above for the turn at hand—while looking all the way to the next turn. That gas, brake, and steering input is supposed to happen in the present but in light of the future.

That future perspective would greatly improve my everyday life. Implementing that skill, all of my emails would be written as though they will be read right before this book or immediately after that Facebook post about my church. That online purchase would take into account a need I could be presented in a few months. The choice between more Instagram scrolling or more FaceTime would consider the legacy I'd like to leave those nieces and nephews. How I explain the bad haircut last time would impact my upcoming conversations with the ladies who cut my hair. Yeah: following a prompt to text someone a few words of encouragement might be inconvenient right now, but that obedience might build relational capital at a future crossroad.

I can't speak for you, but my spiritual journey has been a rally race, not a NASCAR one. Instead of loops around the same track, I've been running stage trials in foreign countries. I'm out on rural roads I've never seen, flying over blind hills and diving into hairpin curves. My suspension has stretched after an unexpected jump. My tires have chirped from hand brake slides. Plastic panels hang off my bumper from bad drifts. I've blown through hamlets and asked, "Did we just miss a cow back there!?"

I've felt over my head and out of control during more weeks than not over the last decade of my life. I need all of these crazy stunts around the world to flush my adrenal system, every once in a while, because of how much my daily realities tax those adrenaline pumps and hoses. It's crazy to me how many times a day my watch vibrates—just to remind me to breathe.

Thankfully, as I learn and grow, I have room for error. So do you. Just like at rally school, we get cones and soft shoulders instead of walls and ditches. The Holy Spirit doesn't get an elevated heart rate watching us approach a curve. Jesus has seen every driver miss his marks. He's watched us all hit the wrong pedal at just the wrongest of times. In his kindness, he has dispatched the tow truck before we even overshot our turns.

At the same time, we should be seeing growth in the process. We should hear God's voice more clearly in the same way I heard Andrew's tenor voice cheering, "There you go!" on more and more turns. Our eyes should be working further and further up the course as rewired instincts and muscle memory take over. As we spend more time with Jesus, our obedience should grow more reliable. Our confessions should happen in quicker and quicker succession. Our heart should pump slower at junctures where it used to race. The Subaru WRX of our life should look more and more to observers like Jesus is driving it.

We don't accomplish this by avoiding slides in life. I'm not sure that's even possible. Our goal is to handle the slides in such a way that others take notice and want some seat time with our Instructor. And when someone asks us about our straight stretches, we'll shrug our answer and add, "But I've done 135 sideways."

BEFORE THE DUST SETTLES

Where do you go when there's no green light?

Nothing prepares you for when the vehicle right in front of you just disappears.

At night.

Crossing a desert.

You can imagine my heart rate as the first one vanished from our convoy. And then the second. No explosions sparked into the wide sky. This isn't a war story. I wasn't playing a video game, riding in a simulator, or navigating through a dream. No: real, actual, raspy exhausts coughed in my face—until they didn't.

I slowed from thirty miles an hour as my insufficient headlights caught only dancing dust on the near horizon. In the far distance, the glow of Las Vegas kept the winter night from drowning us in black. All of a sudden, though, nothing appeared between the end of my hood and the start of those trickling dots. Nothing except dust.

It's interesting to me as I relive this story now that I used the lights on the horizon to orient myself. Vegas doesn't beckon me; it depresses me. I fall as entranced by the Bellagio fountains and Cirque du Soleil acrobatics as the next tourist, but everywhere else emotes an ironic darkness and sadness. The air coats my skin with a film of discomfort, a grimy guilt by association. So, when I've taught seminars in Vegas, I've accumulated a list of excuses to get away from The Strip as much as possible when outside the classroom.

On the night of the disappearing dune buggies, John and I had taken big inhales of clean air out on Bureau of Land Management land a good bit north of town. John sleeps with the windows open year-round in Minnesota, and my thermostat was set in the lake effect snow around an Upstate New York hospital in 1977. So, a December night seemed like a fantastic way to experience a desolate wilderness that bakes its visitors most of the year.

Our guide had told us two things that never left my mind the entire trip. First, he had promised us to keep the gas pedal on the floor as long as we could keep up. John and I each nodded our head in approval and clapped our hands. We would literally be chasing a crazy dude toward the mountains and back as fast as the buggies could go. As the only paying participants on this night, John and I both knew the other wanted to push the limits.

The thrill of that thought got interrupted by the next statement. "Don't roll the buggies. Because of how the oil system works, we'd have to rebuild the motor; we charge you $3,500 for that." The highlight reel of me blasting full speed off the top of a dune suddenly sputtered.

The frames clicked to a stop like the end of an old 16mm reel in a projector. I was more than willing to wreck and roll and tumble down a dune in a five-point harness inside a roll cage, but I wouldn't pay $3,500 for that story.

Thankfully, the guide rarely challenged the balance of our buggies. A large green LED light glowed from atop his lead vehicle. John chased that. I chased John's little red taillight. We jiggled along dry washes and bounced into piles of soft earth that sprayed waves of sand across our faces. Our tires bounced, and every joint of our machines creaked from the pounding. We kept our pedals pressed against the floorboards.

Until the green light disappeared.

That green light fell out of view in front of John. With no radio in our helmets, we got no warning. No signs advised of a precipice. John decelerated a bit but only a bit. His taillight tilted up and at an angle; and then he was gone too.

My eyes widened. I took a big inhale through my nose. My eyes probably widened. For a handful of seconds, I felt suddenly alone. Being strapped into a cage alone in a desert at night—even for a few seconds—shocks the system. So does finding yourself in a spiritual desert. Extended periods in a wilderness of the soul can blanket reality with a lack of hope.

Jesus was just here a few Sundays ago.

I could've sworn he whispered to me in that prayer circle.

I remember feeling him last year at that baptism.

As civilization blinks on the horizon, an ache throbs behind our ribs. A heart once transcendent feels the weight of an unshared sky. In one of those dark nights of the soul, I can't use the sun to determine east and west and then north and south. I need that green light—any green light. What transpired in a few seconds in a Nevada desert has

happened in my life for months at a time, maybe longer. I wish those
seasons all buttoned up as quickly as the dune buggy disappearing act did.

It took only a few seconds on that December night for my hard
tires to crawl to the soft edge of the dune. That $3,500 roll fee flashed
brighter in my mind as I crested the sand. *Don't roll this thing.* Then,
only a second later, I locked onto the taillights at the bottom of the steep
hill and slid down to catch them. *If John didn't roll, I should be good.*

I'm not sure if this is prescriptive or just descriptive, but what I do
at similar spots in spiritual deserts is what I did at the top of that dusty
ledge. I move to where I last saw that light. I slow down and make small,
intentional steps on a trajectory toward where I anticipate Jesus to be.

Those seemingly little movements include reading my journal and
reminiscing on past stories of sovereign infusion. I'll stick around on
a baptism Sunday and listen to an additional service's stories of life
change. Many times, I'll go on a hike in a place where I know nobody
can hear me and describe my pain or worry or confusion out loud.
I can't tell you how many times I retreat to my "Desert Devotions"
playlist on my phone. In "Sing My Way Back," Steffany Gretzinger
describes this reclamation process: "And when I lose direction, when
I can't see the stars—if we get disconnected, I'll sing my way back
to your heart. I'll sing my way back to your arms." Those songs often
warble out of my mouth like from a warped 1980s cassette, as tears
wash my face.

When Sundays—or even months of Sundays—aren't doing the
trick, I still show up. When I don't hear what I want from Jesus when I
want to hear it, I still participate in my weekly Bible studies. When the
horizon seems dark without any green lights, I still don a neon-yellow
vest covered in reflective stripes and wave to parishioners. When I've
lost my way, the voices I can and do hear have a chance to ambush

me, even if for a while they don't. On dunes that can initially feel per-functory, real prayers ring in my ears. From vocal cords I recognize, I hear gentle rebuke and heavy encouragement. Over the years, I've spent a good number of calendar pages going through the motions in church and church-adjacent gatherings; but those environments have often reunited me with the green light again. That community is where I lock back onto Jesus' taillights, where I catch back up.

My Vegas desert guide disappeared because he trusted me and John to follow. His absence came only after John and I had pursued him at full speed across miles of dirt. Jesus trusts those of us who've sought him to find him on the bottom of the next dune too. He promised—in the red letters of the New Testament—that those who seek him will [eventually] find him. My guide wasn't being obnoxious or trying to hide. He wanted to introduce me to a new thrill, a new sensation, a new proficiency in our adventure. He got out in front to stretch me; he pulled out of view to expand my proficiency. He watched intently in his rearview mirror. He left me with a roll cage and thousands of acres. He gave me freedom, knowing I'd try to follow him.

No matter how much dust I've tasted in my wandering, Jesus has always let me back into the convoy. He never offered an angry word, never hit me with an "I told you so," and never asked me "Where were you?" Despite the long stretches I drive between green lights, he never looks at his watch—at least not in front of me. There's always a knowing nod, a welcoming hug. I've never heard it, but I've felt him say, "Welcome back. I missed you." Regardless of how slow I approach the edge of the dune, he still pulls instead of pushes. When I forget Jesus has drawn the topo map of every desert and programmed the GPS for every escape, he puffs up some dust to let me know I'm not alone.

When I lose sight of his LEDs, he reminds me I still have the green light.

MOONLIGHT MASS

Say yes with other people saying yes.

I had always assumed flash mobs had a leader, a plan, and rehearsals—maybe even diagrams. After a fateful night in South Africa, I'm not so sure. Technically, the quasi-impromptu gathering to which I was invited wasn't an official flash mob; but it wasn't a parade or a fundraiser, a protest or a demonstration. Somewhere between 1,000 and 1,500 of us just showed up in the same park at roughly the same time. Nobody was filming an OK Go music video. As far as I know, nobody proposed to their girlfriend at the end of our unsynchronized movement. I never saw a map, a plan, or a schedule, and I had no idea who was leading us. No arches greeted us at the start or finish. I'm not sure there were official lines for either of those.

When we did get to the end, there wasn't room for all of us to congregate; and I didn't hear any mass cheering. So, I stayed long enough to exchange pleasantries and absorb awkward silence before backtracking to roads I could remember and then back to my hostel.

I should back up.

I've stayed in hostels on four continents, but none of them have come close to the one I found in Cape Town's Green Point. On top of some impressive amenities, the people who lived and lodged there proved more inclusive than a multilevel marketing convention. And far more authentic. I enjoyed a *braai* (barbecue) made by an Israeli chef, a sunset hike with an American expat now living in Italy, and an experimental GoPro shoot in the pool with a professional photographer from Germany. Our den mother was a beautiful soul from the Netherlands. The bustle in our breakfast kitchen carried more latent energy than the coffee others were brewing.

One of my new friends from down the hall asked if I'd like her to procure me what she called a "Moonlight Mass bike." I shrugged out a "Sure" and handed her the twelve bucks she said this procurement would require. Later that day, she arrived with a cruiser bike lined with battery-powered lights. After dinner, several of us coasted down the hill to a waterfront park. Hundreds of other cyclists swarmed around us, some in costumes, some wrapped in lights, some with lights mounted on their bikes. As friends found each other in the crowd, the buzz grew until we could see helmets moving. Like when the wave gets to your section at a baseball game, we joined the throng in succession.

We were off.

I never learned whether we had an official police escort or if the sheer mass of independent parts made us too difficult to corral. I vaguely remember us stopping for a traffic light or two. We rolled six or eight wide down secondary streets and then funneled into a single lane on major thoroughfares. No cones. No barricades.

Somewhere in there, we also whizzed down tree-punctuated sidewalks. The night air offset the heat from pedaling and absorbed our January sweat. It also carried music and laughter and giddy shrieks. At any given time, dozens of coasting derailleurs clicked like cicadas. It took me back to riding my BMX bike in one of my childhood driveways under the nocturnal glow of billboards in the adjacent soybean field.

By the look of the faces bobbing around me, we all felt like kids— like the kids in a movie on their way from the swimming hole to the dime store. This summer full moon had to be celebrated. In the home of apartheid, I felt a rightness in the communal aspect of joining hundreds of people from a dozen countries. This Moonlight Mass was described as a monthly gig, and I happened to visit during one of the largest gatherings they'd ever had.

Serendipity.

In the improv game of life, those "yes and" moments have shaped me. When I've said yes to the unknown, those surrenders have eventuated in optimism. When I've left the itinerary in a locked rental car, foreign places have come alive. And so have I. That's not to say any of us should go all Jim Carrey and say yes to everything. Yes isn't always the right answer. It just was the correct response on that Thursday night.

This might sound weird, but that hour in the dark with a gazillion strangers felt something better than special. It held a primal spirituality. Whatever "it" was, it ricocheted within my ribs as a peek at what church could be. My heart reconciled the moment as a secular facsimile of what I've experienced around Jesus people. I've had giddiness spilled on me when we've been running toward God with full cups.

I've been surrounded by "yes and" improvisational ministry. I've watched people of different interests, different politics, and different socioeconomic castes assemble into a haphazard unity, as we moved toward needs. It may have been for only one night or one mission, but we joined our ragtag lights into a moving art piece. We never saw fire fall from heaven, but we often got swept up by an energizing breeze that redeemed our sweat.

These movements have rarely arrived with branded T-shirts. Most haven't come with websites or weeks of church announcements. Those environments have their place, and I've experienced powerful moments in them. But the extemporaneous kingdom sorties didn't originate with the edict of a committee; they didn't need a board to legislate unity. No official lungs tried to breathe life into a program.

Somebody felt a pang or a prompt. That somebody asked at least one other somebody, "What would you think if we moved toward this situation?" Maybe they prayed, or maybe they just knew. Maybe a voice of reason honed their idea with a suggestion or two. "Oh, good thought! Yes: let's do it that way." There wasn't a PowerPoint, a proposal, or a budget submission. Like the first documented church—right after Jesus went back home—my friends brainstormed over meals, passed the hat around, and prayed a blessing over it. In smaller situations where just presence and words were needed, they placed an arm on a shoulder and gave the gift of adjacent silence.

This uneven, organic movement of light captivates bystanders in our stressed-out world as much as it did during the Moonlight Mass. Their eyes follow lighted bikes and lightened souls. They ask questions about a throng of bicyclists and a solitary life well lived. When someone mentions the next Moonlight Mass, they will look around for a bike. When a changed person invites you to what healed them, you might take a flier. Eventually, like I did, the curious will move toward the light and then with it. That proved true of my physical story in Cape Town and my spiritual story back home in Virginia.

People who wouldn't have responded to barking instructors or parade bull horns just might follow their curiosity to something that is as cathartic as it looks. I wouldn't be surprised if random cyclists jumped in with the throng at different points of the full journey that night too. I've definitely seen that happen in my spiritual communities.

It's work to pedal—to move a bike or a life forward. There were Cape Town hills to climb that night just as there are slopes on the topography of life back home. We had to use our brakes and steer around obstacles. We still needed helmets on city streets, just as we need to protect our hearts and thoughts in everyday life. But we were working and staying vigilant in fraternity, empowered by contagious vision. That's not exclusive to impromptu parades in a foreign city. Many of my friends and I have felt tears on our cheeks but also (simultaneously) the weight of hands on our shoulders and prayers in our ears. The "yes and" isn't always fun, but it is moving. My friend, Woody regularly quips, "Whenever God shows up in the Bible—whatever it is, it isn't boring."

For those of you reading this who haven't experienced what I've described, you still can. For those who can only imagine a camaraderie like that, this isn't fiction. One of my friends who has some regrets from prison time and a failed marriage told me after our first few Tuesday nights around a circle together that he knew those of us at the table better than anyone in the religious environment where he'd spent the previous twenty years. A week or two later, a new friend at that same table turned around and told me he had just right then—two feet behind my shoulder—surrendered his life to Jesus after decades of being a spectator.

You can be the catalyst of all of this too—the first yes, the contagious yes. You can play the role of Daniel Graham and Elad Kirshenbaum. "Who are they?" you ask. They are two cyclists who wanted to draw attention to the safety of urban cyclists. They hatched a social experiment on Twitter about a communal bike ride—on full moon nights in Cape Town, South Africa. As they told their friends, those friends responded with "yes and?" and then "YES AND!"

I never biked with that crew again, but I've carried that acceptance and animation with me for years now. The same holds true for my relationships with people with whom I've pedaled in ministry for a proverbial night. We still share that special memory, that eternal moment. Maybe they'll be on my street in heaven; or maybe I'll get to bike past their place on my way to my job up there.

In the meantime, I'll keep saying, "Yes!" to impromptu invites from others saying, "Yes!"

BETWEEN THE CLOUDS

Turns out, you don't need to see where you'll land before you jump.

I had to withhold some details from the following story for legal reasons. International protocol, actually. But I can provide witnesses to corroborate this story if you're skeptical.

After several days of high-altitude backpacking and intestinal distress, I had a few hours free before I had to join my buddies at the train station to start our long journey back to the States. I knew exactly what I wanted to do with that time.

For years now, my research for every vacation has included a Google search with the name of the geographical place and the word *paraglide*. The same was true in the months leading up to that big hiking trek. I got excited when I learned that paragliders from around the world had arrived at that same train station for years, ready to play in the sky overhead. Some liked it so much, they stayed to take tourists like me on tandem rides.

Unfortunately, once I finally made it to this prime paragliding location, it didn't look like I'd be able to make this perennial dream come true. The problem at hand was the same problem we had just faced at our final scenic overlook on the trail: low-hanging cloud cover. Paragliding is governed by visual flight rules (VFR), including visibility requirements. One of those guidelines prohibits takeoff when you can't see the ground.

I had already passed on an epic bungee jump earlier that week. I didn't want to return home without jumping off a mountain too. I know that's an arbitrary requirement, but the heart wants what it wants. So, the stakes were as high for me as the peaks hidden by those clouds. I'd probably never be in this town again, maybe not even this country. We had missed what we were told would be the money shot of the hike. I didn't want to miss the Facebook gold I had hoped to mine with all that extra gear in my pack.

I beelined to the tandem paragliding vendor's office and explained my situation. The pilot, in turn, explained the weather situation. I didn't mind flying through clouds. I wasn't there for the view. Rules are rules, though. I watched the professional paraglider scroll slowly through detailed weather forecasts on his monitor, looking for chances, searching for hope. He explained that we might have a short launch window in a couple hours and took my number. It would be tight to get that in before our train left, but I was willing to take that risk.

About two hours later, I leaped when I got word from the pilot and hurried over to the rendezvous point. I looked up to the sky, hoping for the gray to part. We rode up to the launch site. Anticipation radiated from my face; focus emanated from his. Fog curled and swirled but seemed to be working its way to higher elevations—higher than our 10,000 feet above sea level. Technically, we could see the ground—just not where we wanted to land.

The pilot spread our canopy on the gravel and fidgeted with the lines until they were all straight. I contorted my limbs into my half of the harness. We both leaned into the wind as the paragliding wing pulled taut behind us. It yanked us back two or three steps. Go time. We tugged and chugged across the dirt. Tandem paraglider launches feel somewhere between a three-legged race and one of those two-person horse costumes. Sometimes, there's running. Other times—like on this launch—it looks like a slow-motion replay of running. We hurried in this awkward way until my feet dangled. Then his.

We drifted out over the southeast side of the mountain in the opposite direction of our intended landing spot. Visibility was better over there. By that, I mean there was any visibility at all. As the slope grew farther behind us and as the ground fell off further below us, we floated out across the southern end of the valley. We skimmed along and sometimes through wisps of translucent clouds. For illegal activity, it sure felt like a dream sequence. Sunlight whispered through the moisture and eventually split the clouds, framing the most famous local peak. Serendipity had smiled on us. Both of us returned that smile.

Within a few minutes at most, our canopy had a blue ceiling instead of a gray one. My pilot steered us back toward the train station, twisting below the tree line. We skimmed just over the tops of conifers, while skirting cliffs and contouring along steep slopes. After pulling some G's with spirals and wingovers, we buzzed an unsuspecting hiker and then slid onto the grass behind the train station. He unhooked me from his harness and gathered in the wing. Euphoria on my part and customer service on his part led to a high five.

I don't remember when he told me to keep that whole clandestine launch under wraps. I smirk like Ferris Bueller, though, every time I think of the gift he gave me with that adventure. I assuage my conscience with the technicality that we could see *somewhere* to land the whole time, that at worst we just launched ten minutes too early and that most of the flight wouldn't have drawn the eye of anyone who could enforce negative consequences.

I've always loved the part of commercial flights when the jet pops up over the uneven tops of clouds or weaves around cloudy spires or descends through their wispy bellies. Playing in the clouds in a paraglider turned that exhilaration up to eleven. For the cherry on top, the clouds made the GoPro photos and videos way more epic.

I don't know about you, but I've had a lot of takeoffs in my life where I couldn't see where I would land. I could see a place to ditch, an emergency exit—just not a full view of where I wanted to end up. I went on lots of first dates before I called a girl I had never met and invited her to what would be my last first date. I started a side hustle, not realizing that it would become a corporation and my livelihood for two decades. I joined a parking lot greeter team, not realizing it would lead to the deepest relationships outside of my family. I bought a disc golf starter kit years before my favorite courses were built, years before those wooded walks became my primary cathartic escape from daily stress. In 2001, I got a passport to visit my in-laws on the mission field. I had no premonition or even a realistic intention at that time that I'd visit all seven continents.

On a smaller scale, though, I have similar cloudy spiritual launches several times a week. In short windows of opportunity, I surrender to mystery and leave the landing up to Jesus. They're not always scary, and they definitely don't break any international rules. They arrive as compulsions to text someone a specific message, to write them a card, to invite them to breakfast. I've found out only later that those prompts had been sovereignly timed. Sometimes, the jump is bigger—relinquishing a financial contribution, intentionally engaging in an awkward confrontation, or bringing my counselor into something I'm embarrassed to reveal. More recently, the launches have loomed mountainous: adopting a teenager, confronting a former pastor's sexual abuse, and inviting a friend to give his life to Jesus.

Well. Gulp. *Here goes nothing.*

While the conscience warns us when not to travel outside of beneficial guardrails, Advent calls us to risk something within them. Emmanuel invites us into places where we "see through a glass darkly." Please don't hear a call to foolishness. I'm not recommending you stand on live train tracks or on an interstate in the fog. This isn't a dare to test God's ability to protect you. While Jesus uses martyrs to spread the holistic version of the Gospel, I'm not sure that he conscripts kamikazes. I'm also not saying that you should try to generate a mystery in places where Jesus has clearly shown the way and provided plenty of sunshine to illumine it. The Bible is full of nuance; it doesn't need any extra complication.

A thousand words or so into me writing this chapter, Kobe Bryant's helicopter crashed into a Calabasas hillside. The NBA legend and eight others were flying blind in foggy clouds. I spent some time after that, wrestling with whether I should pull this chapter from the book. I didn't want to hear about a reader doing something stupid and inviting pain or ruin into their life. I didn't want to see a false dream end in smoldering wreckage.

I still don't.

To move past this fork in the road, I had to ask myself, "How do I know when it's Jesus or danger that's shrouded in mystery? How do I differentiate between an unsafe God and unnecessary peril?" For me, one of the biggest filters is whether what I'm about to do is to build my brand or build my obedience quotient. If my ego gains from this jump, that prompt probably didn't come from the Holy Spirit. Because pride constantly whispers in my ear, a heaven-sent compulsion usually requires humility. When I get a silent request at the soul level, it's usually to improve someone else's trajectory or contribute to someone else's prosperity. If an odd urge doesn't contribute to the Kingdom of Heaven, it's probably not from Jesus. It's not that success or convenience is sinful, but Jesus doesn't have to ask us to pursue those things. That's why his signals typically run counter to those natural, magnetic pulls.

You and I will have different clouds—different doubts, different mysteries, different obstacles. Your launches will also leave from different mountains than mine do—different motivations and different definitions of comfortable. Our flight patterns lead to different landing spots too. But personal growth requires discomfort for all of us and in each of us. Spiritual formation happens just outside or way outside of our respective comfort zones. What scares you and what scares me will probably be different, but following Jesus isn't a discomfort competition. Our respective missions and assignments are guided by the common threads of love, grace, mercy, and truth; but they will be expressed and executed in different ways and in different places for different recipients.

Jesus' little brother, James, promised us that his older brother would give us plenty of wisdom when we ask for it. I know how little brothers can be, but I claim that promise more than any other promise written in the Bible. Clouds have made a habit of dancing in the same thermals where I want to play. At the same time, I've found that obedience to those inconvenient whispers has led to some adventures that couldn't have been more perfectly—more sovereignly—scheduled. Small and large moments of surrender have brought about some of the most scenic days of my journey and the most epic rides of my life.

I can't tell you when and where to jump. Half the time, I'm not confident of my own timing and location. My guess is that when you catch one of those tiny launch windows, though, you'll gain a story so incredible you'll feel like you got away with something.

PENGUIN HIGHWAY

Watch where you step.

On my first morning in Antarctica, Tim and Johnny drove a handful of us in a pair of Zodiac boats out to an island a few hundred yards from our blue, ice-dented ship. Huge snowflakes floated around us as if in a silent, choreographed ballet. The mountaineering guides from the United Kingdom tossed some heavy-duty duffels onto the snow. Then they pulled out our ropes and harnesses. Tim free-climbed the ice wall to our left and screwed the top-roping anchor deep into the ice. Johnny distributed our gear and helped adjust some of the straps over our bulky snowsuits. Then, on a tiny island in the Southern Ocean, we took turns climbing an ice face and belaying others from our ship.

Fifteen minutes into this experience, a pair of Adélie penguins swam up to the gravel where we had beached our boats. They watched us like policemen, trying to determine if we were committing a crime or harmlessly loitering. I'm not exaggerating when I tell you that they looked like they were conversing about it, looking at us, cocking their heads, and then making some quip to each other several times. Then, as though with a shrug, they determined we hadn't discovered the door to their speakeasy lair, dove into the water, and disappeared almost immediately. It was the most intelligent thing I observed from any of the scores of penguins I encountered inside the Antarctic Circle.

Because penguins are idiots.

Sure, they're cute; but they're not the brightest bulbs of the Southern Hemisphere. At one stop, we watched male gentoo penguins build stone nests around their baby mommas and future offspring. These pungent ladies stood in incubation posture about ten to twelve feet apart. While their little, gravel volcanoes required impressive construction at some point, the clueless ice roosters just stole their pebbles from each other's nests—passing each other on the way back to their respective wives. With the black and white motif of penguin life, I wouldn't be surprised if the thieves I observed wore nametags labeled Larry, Moe, and Curly.

Maybe they were smart but just pranksters. Regardless, our guides treated the penguin colonies like international airports during the coronavirus scare. Every time we left for shore, we had to dip our Muck boots in a pink disinfectant. And every time we returned to the ship, we repeated this procedure. As hardy as penguins have proven to be in regard to an inhospitable environment, they are apparently utterly fragile in terms of foreign pathogens—even from other penguin colonies.

The preventative care for the penguins continued ashore. In most situations, we wore snowshoes under our soles to spread our weight over a larger surface area and make smaller indentations into the snow.

A bootprint can become a prison for penguins. The flightless birds have no upper body strength and can't use their wings to climb out of imprints we would take for granted. I'm not talking post hole tracks— just regular bootprints. It made sense after explanation. It's not like the other penguins can throw the stranded penguin a safety line and pull him out. Also, an international treaty prevents us tourists from touching them, let alone helping them out of a jam.

Our guides also reminded us to take care around the "penguin highways," the threads of penguin-packed snow that function as the game trails of the Antarctic. Engrossed behind our cameras, it was easy for one of us giants to step on one of their interstates and frustrate their future travel. Photographing the locals for Facebook friends back home could impede their daily life.

We had to pursue adventure in such a way that it didn't hurt someone else's journey.

Journey has grown cliché as a word to describe our spiritual progress in life. It's up there with overused-but-still-useful buzzwords like *season* and *community*. It approaches the saturation levels of phrases like *love on them* and *do life together*. That conceded, we are all moving from a set point to another in life. Well, we should be. With us all fixated on the same horizon and walking in generally the same direction, though, it's too easy to focus on only our own steps. As we walk into new places in life, we default to self-preservation, selfish accomplishment, and then social promotion of our adventure. Unchecked, we turn a walk with Jesus into a race. We repurpose growth into a competition.

That's probably why the early church fathers reminded us of a core tenet of Jesus' mission: caring for those who can't or don't keep up with us. We can't follow Jesus without wearing snowshoes when we go ashore. We can't grow more like Jesus and not walk circumspect of our impact on others. We have to ask ourselves how our choices affect and influence others. We have to listen to observant guides who are calling out needs we might not have considered, the environmentalists who have empathy where we have apathy.

As life travelers, we need to invite those voices into our ears. We need to listen to the talks from people of different ages and ethnicities, those with traumas and obstacles foreign to us. We need to read the books about those intentionally and unintentionally oppressed. We need to absorb podcasts about the destitute and disenfranchised and the systems that exacerbate those situations. We need to sit with the homeless and the addicted, the widowed and the divorced, the abused and the disillusioned. We need to confront our ignorance and our arrogance.

And then we need to dip our daily practices in the basin of pink stuff. We need to scrub our sermons and social media posts with the accompanying boot brushes. We've got to ensure we don't carry our whiteness, our wealthy-ness, or our American-ness to different cultures. We've got to understand that our privilege extends beyond the obvious to places like body chemistry, serendipity, and family of origin. What works for us doesn't work for everybody, and we don't know better than the people who work in those environments.

When I've realized that Jesus gave me my blessings for his kingdom instead of mine, I've had to wrestle with how I leverage those blessings. I mean, how carefully and intentionally did Jesus live with us penguins? He spent his entire life in snowshoes. He knew we couldn't get ourselves out of bootprints—and definitely not by proverbial bootstraps.

Then he told us, "Go, and do likewise."

If this sounds like extra work, that's because it is. But the ensuing reward is at least equal to that hassle and discomfort. At times, it stinks like a penguin colony during nesting; but you get to stand in places few ever have. When you forego alcohol at a barbecue in deference to a friend who struggles with moderation, you both get to enjoy the cookout more. When you intentionally avoid words or jokes that trigger someone's past trauma, you create relational capital, which can lead to kingdom wins.

The same goes for asking questions of a friend to know where their beneficial boundaries lie. When you humbly engage with those from different backgrounds, both of your horizons expand. When you ask questions instead of pointing fingers, you get more friends and deeper relationships. When you practice what Jesus' brother called "true religion" by caring for widows and orphans, you feel connected to something bigger than yourself. When you expand the radius to include religious and political refugees and those recovering from abuse or bad choices, you feel connected at least to legacy and at most to infinity.

We don't have to apologize to the penguins in our lives for building more immunities or for being tourists. It's healthy for both sides of the equation to take notice of the preexisting structures and life experiences that created cultural differences. We are all products of the environments from which we've journeyed, and we need to tread carefully when exploring each other's worlds. On the flip side, we also don't need to apologize for being a penguin, for having limitations or vulnerabilities in our physical, financial, emotional, relational, or spiritual realities. Given enough time, each of us will take turns on both sides of the tourist-penguin continuum.

People who don't know Jesus are watching how we handle that tension and the friction those differences cause. That's why Jesus asked his father and ours to help us stand in unity—so that spectators would recognize Jesus as God and see us as recipients of divine love. That's a tall order, almost impossible this side of heaven. But when we get it right, even for the equivalent of a day's worth of snowshoeing in Antarctica, people take notice. When we take care of others like Jesus took care of us, we inspire wonder. Even as penguins, our unity can make an inhospitable place look like a great ecosystem in which to live.

RIGHT SIDE UP

You're still here for a reason.

My wife somehow missed being decapitated by a road sign.

I pass that sign every morning on the way to work—because it hangs next to the stairs to my office. I found it in the snow near where our 1990 Cutlass Supreme had flipped end-over-end before rolling five times. I wouldn't have believed we had been upside down six times had I not counted the alternating imprints of our roof and wheels in the snow. I walked away with a scrape on my ankle and two damaged discs in my lower back. My wife suffered less than that. Neither of us was wearing seat belts because mine didn't work, and she had just removed hers to apply last-minute makeup before church. No airbags deployed. Back in 2001, $700 first cars didn't come with them. While airborne, our car snapped that sign's post in half. That sign should've pierced Crystal's window. I should've found a horrific consequence. Instead, she bounced off the inside of the windshield and landed on the shifter—almost in my lap.

The tumult ended with our Oldsmobile back on its wheels—engine still running—facing the opposite direction. When the frenzy stopped, Crystal exclaimed, "Turn it off!" Maybe we both pictured the car exploding like in the movies, or maybe that was just me. We scurried from the car, just in case. The driver of the minivan I had been preparing to pass saw everything through his rearview mirror and returned to the scene to see if we had even lived. We didn't own a cell phone. Apparently, he didn't, either. So, he walked us across the rural highway to a stranger's house to call for the police, arrange a tow truck, and request a ride.

I can't remember, but I think we hitched a ride to church instead of home.

The sign has sharp edges that still make me cringe. It's one of those square, yellow signs with a giant sideways v that can be a greater-than symbol or a less-than symbol—to warn you to turn right or left. The night I retrieved it, I took the sign—and the half of its post still bolted to it—to our church's midweek prayer service and placed it behind the pastor's lectern. He looked aghast as I leaned it against the wall, but I wanted the handful of parishioners around us to understand the gratitude behind my prayer that night.

My voice cracked as I said something about my life-changing direction. Between you and me, it felt profound to say; but I'm not sure what I was foretelling. I would never have imagined then how that prophecy has proven true. Within half a decade, I launched both a new company and a pursuit of adrenaline rushes around the globe. I moved from the flat horizons of Indiana to Virginia's mountains void of straight or level roads. I transitioned from a small white church to a tiny Hispanic church to a church where four thousand people have attended on an Easter weekend. I replaced sedans in my life with coupes, an apartment with a mortgage. I moved on from two college awards to more than two hundred professional ones.

I'm not sure wrecking my car and almost killing my wife caused any of that—let alone all of it. But all of that was a gift I didn't deserve.

Not long after landing right side up in a Collins Corners field, I do remember thinking, *I'm still here for a reason. God's not done with me yet.* At twenty-three, that's kind of an odd thought. I mean, how many recent college grads don't have a lot of life left to live, destinies to fulfill? What holder of youth and health, education and marketable skills doesn't have an opportunity to make a run at kingdom impact, the American Dream®, or both?

I'm almost twice that age now, and I shake my head over all I would've missed if either or both of us hadn't survived that wreck. I think about the lives we've seen changed since then—including our own. I think about the souls who've been baptized, the sheep who've been shepherded, and the relationships that have been repaired. I think about what I've watched Jesus do in and around me and especially through Crystal. All of that fits into a black arrow on a yellow square.

I've had other flashbacks to moments where Fortune smiled on me, where I cheated death, where a rescue arrived just in time. I shudder, recalling a time in the next car I owned after that Oldsmobile when I just missed ramming my wife's side of the car into a parked vehicle at seventy miles per hour. I think about sleepwalks that could've ended badly, including the one where I was outside our Tennessee house which fronted on a four-lane road. I think about the nights I've slept on cliff ledges despite my propensity for that sleepwalking.

If guardian angels are a thing, I've helped a few sweat through their T-shirts. I'm still here. For the record, I'm trying to keep it that way. I'm not sure which second chance I'm on now. Should there be a record of that available in the next life, I'll definitely be looking that up—especially if there's video playback.

"Hey, can I see that from the other camera angle?

In slo mo?

Man! That was close.

Whew! Good save there."

I just hope that folder doesn't also include a record of the opportunities I've wasted. If it does, I'll be too ashamed after looking at my new regrets to ask for anyone else's folder. Since that morning when our Oldsmobile stuck a Simone Biles-level landing, I've spent time upside down in my health, my finances, my employment, and my relationships. Sometimes, I've had more than one of those inversions going at the same time. Fittingly, I've often landed wrong side up in areas where I had recently taken too much credit for success. God doesn't just resist the proud; he flips their scripts. He does mine, anyway. I can't speak for other pride addicts, but apparently, I have to be regularly reminded that my life wasn't spared to spend it on me. My ego didn't save me. Neither did my accomplishments. Sovereignty did.

Philosophers debate the meaning of life. Theologians wrestle with the balance of free will and divine intervention. I'm not qualified to answer those questions. Candidly, you probably shouldn't trust any existential declarations from someone who's tried to cross a pond on the back of a snowmobile—during a *June* family reunion. That said, we all know we're still on this planet for something more than existence. We've all looked at a night sky and felt the weight of infinity on our lack thereof. We've all felt the pull to surrender to something greater than ourselves.

We've all been given a second chance. We all have a backstory. We all have an address in the Your Location box of our Google Maps that's different from the Destination box. We all have the ability to leverage the rest of our life for something bigger than our life.

No matter which translation of the Bible you read, you'll find it filled with people living out second chances: Abraham, Sarah, Joseph, Moses, Samson, Ruth, David, Peter, Paul, and Dorcas. Oh, and that crazy, naked dude who'd been living in a graveyard. I don't have hard data on this, but it seems like Scripture highlights more screwups and former screwups than it does tidy protagonists. It's comforting to know we share the fallibility of the greats of the faith.

Not all who were given second chances in the Bible used them well. Some wasted their gifts of extended grace and extra time. Major characters like Noah, Lot, and Saul failed to write better stories in the later chapters of their books. Jonah did move toward redemption and then didn't. Hezekiah fumbled his extended life. Those cautionary tales remind us that a longer life isn't automatically a fuller one. We can spend our gift cards on poor purchases. In his kindness, Jesus has given many of us bonus days even when he knows we will waste them.

We're all playing in overtime. If we're alive, we have an assignment. If we're breathing, we still have opportunities for kingdom influence. If we're right side up, we can still walk away from our wrecks. Whether we're on our second chance or our fortieth, we can make 'em count. If we've survived Collins Corners, we should live for the One who saved the rest of our lives.

THE MENU

Try the items outside of your comfort zone.

I live less than ten minutes from Candlers Mountain. I'm not sure that it introduces itself as a mountain at parties. Its summit stands only about 1,300 feet above sea level, according to my hiking apps. Candlers is nowhere near the tallest mountain where I live, but it gets you up over everything in between you and the real mountains. It holds many perfect perches to watch the sun set over those real peaks—the front range of the Blue Ridge Mountains. Under its trees, Candlers holds two championship disc golf courses and more than fifty miles of dirt trails and fire roads. I spend a lot of time on all of the above, especially when I'm training for upcoming backpacking trips.

I love daybreak up there.

I was hiking up there before breakfast a few Februarys ago, wearing a weighted vest and some headphones. As the sun got ready to rise, fog sneaked between the trees. At one point, my eyes got moist; and I punched the air while reflecting on an answered prayer. White-tailed deer hopped across the leaves below the trail while I reveled in the distance from my email inbox and my task list.

After descending Candlers Mountain, I walked into our local Cracker Barrel with disheveled hair and sweat patches on my shirt. As expected, my friend Nancy smiled from behind the counter. She hit the buzzer for the kitchen to bring out my order, and I explained that I had been hiking up on the mountain in the beautiful mist and thought I deserved meat for breakfast.

I won't soon forget her powerful response.

"There is adventure in you!"

These weren't the words of a Tony Robbins-like motivational speaker. Her proclamation didn't resound like those of Martin Luther King, Jr. or the "you get a car!" version of Oprah. Robin Williams wasn't yelling it to a classroom or Will Hunting.

No. Nancy's voice slipped out of her smile like Karen Trust Grassle used to deliver her lines as Caroline Ingalls in *Little House on the Prairie*. The words seemed sweet to her soul—as if she were amused by the thought.

To me, hiking on a well-worn, sign-guided trail at sunrise didn't register as an adventure. Maybe it should have. Maybe I have grown calloused. More than likely, though, it's just that I define adventure differently than Nancy does.

And you probably define adventure differently than either Nancy or I do. If you're like me, your definition and measurement of adventure have changed over time too. We define love differently at different times in our lives. The same goes for your interests and what you think is fun or cool.

It's okay that we all have different definitions and expressions of adventure. We were wired that way, just as we were given different love languages, different spiritual pathways, and different kingdom gifts. No two of us are identical. Even the same combinations of interests and abilities can land at different points on the adventure continuum.

Actually, you'll find multiple spectrums of adventure in life. While I'm probably on the bolder side of the physical adventure scale, I'm relatively timid on the other gamuts. My wife would never paraglide with me, but she regularly proves herself more relationally adventurous than I'll ever be. Her sister, Ruby, is more culturally adventurous than most Americans, including me. My buddy, Mitch, enjoys gastronomical adventures that trigger my gag reflex. He's built like an NFL lineman, but he was nervous (as I would be) following my wife into the red-light district of Managua to shower kindness on prostitutes. My family is filled with as many vocationally adventurous people as you'll find in your local chamber of commerce. My friends, Josh and Judson, are as artistically adventurous as a full season of *America's Got Talent*. Day traders go on more intentional financial adventures than I ever plan to go. Many of my friends pursue more spiritual adventures than I've embraced.

You get the idea.

Adventure is found in exploring, trying new things, pushing past our individual comfort zones. While age, influence, and experience cause individual levels of adventure to fluctuate, I would dare say Nancy could have made her declaration to many of the people who attend our shared church. We all have some adventure in us, even if nascent.

If you're a parent, you're on an adventure—and not just when you're trying to find a bathroom to avoid a child's accident. If you drive a school bus, know that I look up to your adventurous occupation. If you work at Chick-fil-A, I don't need to tell you how wild your job can be. If you lead a church, a classroom, or a sports team, you know that leadership is a grand expedition. My friends who parent foster kids are more courageous than I'll ever be. If you take artistic risks, if you put yourself out there for love or friendship, or if you do the uncomfortable thing to resolve conflict, you're an adventurer.

If you lean into the promises Jesus made, you're brave. If you trust him with a tithe of your income, you're courageous. If you hold to his parameters for sexuality, you're daring. If you hand your worries to him, you're audacious. If you honor the concept of sabbath, you're a daredevil in our consumer culture. If Jesus lives in you and has access to your will, adventure ricochets around your soul.

We all get moments of truth where we stand at a line in the sand between "I've never" or "I can't" and "I just did." If we want to grow closer to Jesus or even just follow him from our current distance, we'll walk through those thresholds time and time again. Growing up in physical life is an adventure. Why would the spiritual journey to full maturity be anything less?

Adventure is a muscle, and it can be exercised. Like physical training, it's often easier to push your boundaries in an accountable community. If you don't have local adventurers—people in your lane of exploration—take heart. There has never been a better time for finding those who share your passion. You can connect via Facebook groups, co-op newsletters, and clubs. You can follow Instagram hashtags or bloggers. You can get notified of meetups and conventions. You can engage with Twitter subcultures. The sky's the limit.

I regularly get asked how I got into adventuring, how I find such exciting experiences all over the planet. My go-to answer is that I've surrounded myself with adventurers. These people call out to the adventurer in me and invite me along on their bold and crazy journeys. They know my legs might tremble, that my stomach might be in my throat; yet they don't let my fears keep me from missing out on incredible moments.

This is true of both physical adventures and spiritual ones. I'm embarrassingly blessed with men and women who will challenge me to radical obedience. I'm inspired by friends who make great sacrifices for Jesus, who climb mountains of perseverance, who traverse raging rivers of hardship. They dig into Jesus' words like an Indiana-Jones-level archeologist. Guys with diverse jobs and varying displays of facial hair challenge me with how they embrace discomfort for supernatural unity.

My life is richer for finding camaraderie in the silos of my interests, yet I'm a better human because of exposure to a diverse group of people with a mosaic of passions. I am more firmly rooted in the soil of God's kingdom because his explorers and cartographers freely share what they've found. I am closer to Jesus because of peer pressure to join the expedition and then stay on it. I would hope that other journeyers would say the same because of my contribution. The blueprints Jesus drew for the church look like this whole deal was designed to work through contagious and symbiotic relationships. One of the first-century scribes summed it well with the command to "spur each other to good works."

I'm regularly inspired in my adrenaline pursuits by seeing others absorb the fruit of their risks. I'm amazed by brothers and sisters who exchange comfort for purpose. I'm challenged by loved ones who I see sacrifice their will and their comfort for the good of another. With some bars of cell service, decent Wi-Fi, or moments of extroversion, you can find similar inspiration.

Or you can walk into the Wards Road Cracker Barrel before work on a Wednesday morning. Ask for Nancy.

THE STORIES WE SHARE

Which Tripadvisor pictures do you trust?

Driving out to lunch after church one afternoon, I scanned through my radio station presets. I stopped when I heard a local radio preacher talking about skydiving. The well-mannered orator didn't strike me as the skydiving type. He confirmed that when he interjected, "Now, I've never jumped out of a plane." To be fair, you don't need to have fallen through the sky to understand how skydiving demonstrates concepts like faith and dependence and abandon.

He asserted that faith isn't just believing a parachute works from the comfort of the ground or even the plane. He explained that faith in that parachute is expressed only when you jump. As someone who has both skydived and used the same analogy in discussing my journey with Jesus, I can tell you he wasn't wrong.

What struck me about his sermon illustration is that I had heard it at my church that very morning. My city is currently big enough for only one airline to serve our airport, but we can choose from—I kid you not—several *hundred* churches. So, it's not surprising that two different pastors in my area would be talking to their congregations about faith on the same day. Both pastors using skydiving on the same morning and me hearing both seemed odd enough to ask myself what Jesus was trying to tell me.

I was struck by the uncanny convergence of these two moments. I was wowed by the juxtaposition of seemingly similar presentations. But the whisper in my soul was a call to consider how they differed.

Before I explain that, you have to know my pastor isn't known for his stage presence. Woody dislikes public speaking, despite more than forty years of acclimating to it. You won't find him on the radio or TV. Frankly, I've been impacted more by his teaching off stage than I have from his words on stage—which makes sense when you consider his masters thesis focused on experiential education. He has spent years of his life in the desert and mountains and wilderness, leading backpacking trips and river experiences. He taught me how to find, meet, and commune with God in nature. He has been close during many of the literal and figurative desert moments of my soul.

Don't get me wrong. The pastor I heard on the radio is the real deal too. He has lived a life above reproach despite great scrutiny. He is a humble man whose passion for Jesus and the gospel cannot be questioned. He shepherds members of my extended family and many good souls in my community. He is careful with his words, gentle with his manner, yet undeterred in pursuit of what's right. His church's local and global ministry partnerships are making great strides in addressing the brokenness in the lives of addicts, the fatherless, and the less fortunate.

Both of these men follow God well. Both are building enviable legacies. Both afflict the comfortable and comfort the afflicted. Both make the Bible more approachable. Both hold doctorate degrees and lead megachurches. Both let others have the limelight. Both take their responsibilities seriously and make sacrifices for the kingdom of heaven.

But only one has jumped out of a plane.

I know, because I was there when he jumped.

In fact, I jumped out of the same plane.

Our social media streams, television panels, and conference podiums are filled with people telling stories that aren't their own. What the speakers are saying isn't necessarily wrong or deceitful. You can be right but still not have experienced the truth for yourself. Speaking in the theoretical isn't inherently wrong, either. Fables and parables can bring helpful clarity. Statistics and apologetics can give audiences frameworks for understanding. Philosophical debates can be fun. Creeds have guided religious people for centuries.

The stories we share make a greater impact, though, when they're our own stories.

A thousand men can tell you about childbirth. They can all be physicians—even all obstetric doctors. But none of those male practitioners can speak on how that process physically and emotionally feels. None of them can fully explain the connection a mother has with her unborn baby or her delivered child. But your mom is an expert, and so is mine.

Every single person we meet is drawn to people with real stories and relatable lives. They don't want someone to tell them, "Jesus will redeem this pain." They want someone who says, "This is how God has shown up in my pain." Your friends don't want to hear, "Just have faith." They're waiting for the day when a person of faith says, "This is where I doubted God—when I didn't think he was who he said he was. But this is what I learned about God during that traumatic time."

We all want to hear first-hand stories from people whose eyes glow while telling them. We all give more credence to people who've struggled, who've overcome, who've lived out of their convictions. We all trust suggestions from people who buy what they're recommending with their own money. When a pastor's on stage, we all prefer that he show us his skydive video instead of tell us a theoretical illustration he hasn't personally tested.

Faith is far more than just believing the right stuff. It's living the right stuff—often outside of our comfort zones. Faith acts on the stories others have told us, whether those others are the guys who penned the Bible or people we know who've lived the Bible's claims. Faith works best in proximity to its need, not from an intellectual distance. Faith cashes the checks Jesus wrote instead of re-auditing his records.

If you want to make an impact or build a legacy, you won't accomplish either of those goals in assent or intentions. You'll find it a hundred feet below the plane you just left—not on the ground. You'll find it where the people don't look like you. You'll learn about it from folks who don't make the assumptions you do. You'll grow it around people who don't appreciate you.

If you want to influence the world around you, you have to keep moving. You have to push your way to places where the discomfort will lead to stories you can later remind yourself and tell others about. Bob Goff says it best: "If you want more faith, do more stuff." And if you want others to experience your faith, you have to show them a real, live, relatable version of it.

The people in our lives do the same thing in real life that I do on Tripadvisor. I look at the "Traveler" photos before I book a hotel. I want to learn what people who weren't paid to stay or take pictures there experienced. I want to know the real deal. I search for the reviews that speak to the things I care about in a place to sleep and shower.

The value of authenticity is part of why sharing our faith stories is so important. We all have different stories to which only certain other people will relate. Some will be fellow skydivers. Some will be fellow mamas. Jesus gave each of us a unique collection of passions, friends, and challenges. He loves the people who will have things in common with us at a moment in time when they also need to have our faith in common.

Between you and me, for the most part, I hope you don't tell people the stories from this book. I'm sharing these stories with you, in case they work as Tripadvisor "Traveler" photos for you. I hope the stories you're telling friends and family and coworkers are *your* stories. You don't have to jump out of a plane or push a baby out of your belly to own impactful stories. I've been inspired by my friends' tales from grocery stores and construction sites. I've clapped my hands with excitement while listening to stories from hospital rooms and cubicle farms. Faith has come alive to me through moments shared in the cab of a truck and at a table in Cracker Barrel.

When God is doing something new, you might recognize it through laughter or tears, goosebumps or sweat. It might arrive with a raucous celebration or quiet exhales. Whatever your faith journey looks like, realize that it's uniquely yours. But it's only yours so that it can be retold in your voice to someone who needs to hear it—from you.

To do that, you'll have to live the stories before you can tell them. At the same time, they're only stories if you share them. Whatever jumping out of a plane is for you, do it. And then tell people how you met God in that experience.

ACKNOWLEDGMENTS

Normally, this is the place where the author thanks people in their life for helping them get their book out into the world. I've already thanked those folks individually, often repeatedly, and (where possible) in-person. In case you don't count Jesus as part of the "people" category, don't worry. I've talked to him more than anyone else about this book—most often on the trails of Candlers Mountain.

So, I'd like to use this part of the book to acknowledge the places where it was shaped. (This list is safer since places don't care if you forget them on a public list.)

First, I want to mark the emotional place where the manuscript started. I typed the first words of *Scared to Life* on Friday night, June 8, 2018—the day the world learned that Anthony Bourdain had taken his life in a Paris hotel room. Thanks to the advice of Bob Goff and

Jen Koech, only a handful of the words from that original introduction made the final draft; but Bourdain's death helped launch this book. I didn't follow his work or watch his shows. I'm not an adventurous eater, unless you consider chicken nuggets and tater tots for breakfast as exotic. (I eat them with spaghetti sauce and shredded mozzarella, in case that sways your opinion.)

As a curious world traveler, though, I wrestled with how his global adventures had left him empty and whether my international adrenaline rushes felt empty too. As I flipped back through my Facebook albums and travel blog posts, though, I was overcome by how much Jesus had infiltrated my expeditions, how much the Holy Spirit had ambushed me where I ran to escape pain, and over how many time zones the Father had chased my heart.

These 60,000± words and the thousands more deleted along the way joined each other in sporadic doses and in unrelated places. I've typed pages of this manuscript from the front seats of my MINI Cooper ("Hutch"), my MINI Countryman ("Hank"), and aisle seats on planes. I've pecked out paragraphs while sitting in camp chairs and on picnic blankets, on boulders and on block walls, in beds and in my pillow pit, on weathered benches and on the floor. I've huddled over this keyboard in restaurants and coffee shops, next to rivers and creeks, in a tiny house and in a loft apartment, in hotel rooms and at the top of a 17-story glass tower. I even pounded out two or three chapters in the swanky terminal of a seaplane airport. Writing sabbaticals in Portland, Oregon, and Vancouver, British Columbia, supplied heaping helpings of chapters but not as many as stolen hours did in Evington, Lynchburg, and Tyro, Virginia.

This book is an altar of sorts, but not in your phone or wherever your print edition sits. This compilation stands as a scattered memorial in places as common and unassuming as parking lots. Its stones were gathered from disparate places and stacked in yet others. I don't ever want to forget all of the diverse locations where I heard eternal whispers while transcribing thoughts that often had never occurred to me before those serendipitous moments. And I want you to know that Jesus speaks in commonplace settings and just about anywhere we intentionally quiet our souls. Whether you share those discoveries online or not, publicly or not, eloquently or not, I hope this book encourages you to transcribe your personal and spiritual discoveries—those moments when Heaven gifts you with wonder or awareness, clarity or inspiration. I hope you go back and re-read what you wrote, whether that's in a journal, in a blog post, on social media, or even in a book of your own. Whether you're scared or not, I hope your search for eternal truth leads you to as much life as my search has gifted me.

The author's proceeds of this book will be donated to Love Does. Love Does fights for human rights and provides education to women and children in conflict zones. You can contribute to what Jesus is doing through this incredible organization at

www.lovedoes.org

If you liked Ryan's stories of physical adventure and spiritual discovery, you can find more at

www.explorience.org

Ryan interviews adventurers he has met in his travels on the Everyday Adventures podcast. Look for it wherever you listen to podcasts or at

www.podcastfriends.com

The editing, design, and audio adaptation of this book were sponsored by Biplane Productions, Inc. Since 2002, Biplane has helped auction companies look like marketing experts to their sellers. Biplane has contributed to the marketing campaigns of 8,500 auctions in 49 states and 7 foreign countries, winning 250 state, national, and international advertising awards in the process. Biplane's clients have made it possible for Ryan to pursue the adventures in this book.

www.biplaneproductions.com